Excel VBA in simple programming

An easy and quick course

Cacildo Marques

ISBN: **978-1981391011**

Marques, Cacildo
Excel VBA in simple programming: an easy and quick course/
Cacildo Marques.
EpistemeEd , 2017.

80p.

ISBN: 978-1981391011

I. Computer Programming. I. Titles   CDD 005

CONTENTS

Alert

This is a simple, step-by-step, but at the same time deep programming course for anyone who wants to get started on the subject and is not satisfied to just stay on the surface. It serves high school students, engineers, physicists, chemists, economists, architects, mathematicians, students of exact sciences, biomedical sciences and various humanities.

Because Excel is on all Windows computers, everyone who owns the machine can learn programming by simply following the paths indicated in this volume.

Many people recommend Basic programming not to be introduced to beginners, because the features of this language can further prevent the mastery of more formal codes, such as Pascal, C, and Ada. This may be true when the manuals used by the learner depart from whom does not know other languages or, even knowing them, does not respect the fundamental rules of those.

The present course is structured in order to prepare the reader for later knowledge of other languages without any blocking, since there are, in fact, two levels of Basic: one popular, relaxed, and another rigorous, beautiful and academic, even maintaining the characteristic simplicity of the language. Let us embrace this second version.

The author.

Excel VBA in simple programming

An easy and quick course

Cacildo Marques

Chapter 0 Introduction

Beginning. Before programming properly in Excel, the user usually has access first to the spreadsheet, in which he can obtain a multitude of results, either through simple operations or through more complicated procedures.

The first information that a beginner should receive when faced with a blank spreadsheet and wants to make some account is how he should enter his data. It is not enough, as one would imagine, to write the account and press Enter. Let us suppose that the user wants to get the value of a multiplication, for example 38 * 42.5. If he types in this way, he will get no response. It must start with the equality symbol, "=". So he should do, in any cell:

= 38 * 42.5

Done! Pressing Enter the result will come, and the beginner will be able to do any elementary account in the worksheet.

The symbols of the operations are:

OPERATION	SYMBOL	EXAMPLE
Addition	+	= 2 + 3
Subtraction	-	= 18 - 7
Multiplication	*	= 7 * 15
Division	/	= 105/35
Power	^	= 5^3
Square root	sqrt	= sqrt(400)

You must also know the relationship operators used in Basic. These are as follows:

NAME	BASIC	PURE MATHEMATICS
Equal	=	=
Greater than	>	>
Lesser than	<	<
Superior or equal to	>=	≤
Inferior or equal to	<=	≥
Different	<>	≠

The user may want to use several cells in his calculations, and this is very easy. If he wants to put a value in the cell B2 (column B, row 2), another in the cell C3, with the result of some operation he decides appearing in the cell A4, then he will type, for example, 28 in the cell B2, 46 in the cell C3 and = (B2 + C3)/2 in the cell A4. The result obtained in this last cell will be the arithmetic mean of the contents of the two previous cells.

From the two examples above, calculation in a cell and calculation using several cells, the novice user can look for numerous other examples of use of spreadsheet and can consult the program Help to perfectionate himself and extend the knowledge, always practicing each information received .

Preparing. When entering the Excel VBA (Excel Visual Basic Applications) programming environment, one can choose to build and run a stand-alone program, such as it was in QBasic, QuickBasic, Algol and Clipper, and it is still today in Visual Basic, Visual C++ and Delphi, among others, or he can build a procedure to interact with any worksheets on which it is working.

At the beginning of the history of microcomputers there were few ready programs in stores, and users, because of this, had to program if they wanted to give wide use to their machines. Thus, the operating system of the computers already presented, in an ostensive way, its interpreters or compilers, so that the user could program. The IBM-PC of the early eighties, for example, came with DOS, its operating system, equipped with BASIC, the interpreter negotiated with Bill Gates, founder of Microsoft. Bill Gates, on the other hand, had previously acquired DR-DOS from a fellow Seattle native, then he adapted the BASIC language to that environment. The original BASIC is a language created in 1964 by John Kemeny for mainframe computers, at a time when there were still no microcomputers, which only came to light in 1975.

Because programming is no longer a necessity of most computer users, the programming environment is no longer evident in machines. When you install the Office suite, containing Excel, the Visual Basic environment does not appear on the screen. It is necessary for the programmer to search for it in the hidden devices of the system and bring it to the menu of the spreadsheets environment.

Doing this is very easy. From Excel 2010, for going to the Developer button the user should click on the File menu, Options. In the dialog box, click Customize Ribbon. On the right side, check the Developer box. Done! Just give Enter to Ok.

Looking at the menu, the user will see on the right side the Developer tab. Clicking there, just choose Code, or Visual Basic. (In older versions of Excel, when the pprogramming area was already on the menu, simply click the Tools tab, Macro, and then choose Visual Basic Editor.)

Being in the spreadsheet environment, one should save the file one wants to work with, giving it a name, for example, MyProg.

Module. Going to the VBA programming environment, through the Developer menu, if the code window is not open, the programmer clicks the "Insert Module" icon arrow, which comes after the "View Microsoft Excel" icon under the top of the menu Archive. After clicking the arrow, a few options appear, and the "Module" line must be clicked, to display the blank code window with the name of the file, "MyProg", or another one that has been chosen, followed by Module1 , on the blue top stripe. At this point, the developper should go to the File menu and save what

3

has already been done. To go from the spreadsheet environment to the programming environment, the user can choose a keyboard shortcut: just press the Alt and F11 keys at the same time.

To create a program that generates a numeric or alphanumeric value, we write the code between the reserved words that appear: Function and End Function. After the word Function, we give a name to the program, and then the type of variable in which the result should come, whether integer (*Single*, *Integer* or *Long*), whether rational (*Decimal* or *Double*), whether alphanumeric (*String*), etc. A more elastic variable declarative is *Variant*, which we use when we are not sure what kind of output can come out, or when we want the variable to have behavior of one kind or another, depending on the moment of use. There is also a variable declaration that the programmer can create, using the declarative *Type*, using a *Type - End Type* loop, but the reader does not have to worry about it now.

If we want as a result some procedure other than a single, numeric or alphanumeric result, we use the words *Sub* and *End Sub* to open and close our program.

A first program, to recalculate the arithmetic mean of two fixed numbers, can be written as:

```
Function Average1( )
      Rem Sample Program 1a
      a=9
      b=14
      x=(a+b)/2
      Average1=x
End Function
```

When saving the program, via the File menu, and returning to the worksheet, also through the File menu, the user will see the result after entering a cell with any expression =Average( ) and click Enter. The reserved word *Rem*, in the second line of the program, comes from Remark, i. e., observation. It serves to initiate comments, which will not be processed in the program, but

4

only registered.

For all the examples presented in this book, it is of fundamental importance that the reader does not copy and paste the code into the programming environment, but that he comes to enter it step by step, to get accustomed to all the symbols involved.

When the reader typed Function, followed by the name of the program given by the user, Average1( ), immediately after pressing Enter the program left a blank line and presented the final line, End Function. These two words and also the initial word, Function, had their color changed to blue, indicating that they are reserved words of the Basic language, which in our case is Excel VBA. Reserved words are in the language library and cannot be used by the programmer with another porpose and cannot function as variables, for example. Whenever we enter a reserved word, Basic immediately introduces it with an initial capital letter. If it does not change the color to blue, it's just a library function. So in our examples, these words are capitalized, but the user must type them in lowercase so that he can verify that they are automatically capitalized after the line change, which is a way to check if they are typed correctly. If, after entering and changing, the reserved word continues with lowercase initial, something went wrong and deserves attention.

In the blank line, after Function Average1( ), the reader was typing the four lines of code that completed the program. These lines could be typed all in one line, separating the instructions not with a semicolon, as it is done in several other languages, but with two points, thus giving the program:

```
Function Average1( )
    a = 9: b = 14: x = (a + b) / 2: Average1 = x
End Function
```

The above program is one of the most simplified that the user can create. Two values are assigned to two variables, and then a formula uses these variables to find a value, which in this case is the arithmetic mean. This value is assigned to the function name, which operates as a final variable. When returning to the

5

spreadsheet environment and running the created application, the reader can never forget to type "=" before the program name, if it is a function.

Declaring. In programming languages in general, the user is required to make a variable type declaration to be used at the beginning of the program or in the internal block of that program. Basic offers some facilities, among them that of skipping the declaration. It is advisable, however, that the beginner is accustomed to declare variables, since this is the general pattern.

While rewriting the previous program, we will use the reserved word As, for the function itself, and *Dim* for the internal variables of the code, besides the type of variable, which can be *Boolean, Byte, Sbyte, Char, Short, Integer, Long, Single, Decimal, Double, String, Variant, Currency* and *Date*, each with an extension, i. e., a size. Byte, for example, goes from 0 to 256, while Integer goes from -32768 to +32767, Single goes from -3.4E38 to +3.4E38 and Double goes from -1.79E308 to +1.79E308 ("E" means here "Times 10 raised to"). The word Dim, always placed at the beginning of the statement, comes from "dimension." We can have, for example:

```
Function Average2( ) As Double
    Rem Sample Program 1b
    Dim a, b, x As Integer
    a = 9
    b = 14
    x = (a + b) / 2
    Average2 = x
End Function
```

Modification: Change the numbers 9 and 14 to other values.

The Dim statement can be used inside the program to declare several types of variables. In three consecutive lines we can, for example, declare **n** as integer (Dim n As Integer), **y** as rational of

6

double size (Dim and As Double) and **ana** as alphanumeric (Dim ana As String).

In common algebra, a variable is a single letter, such that, if we use more than one character, the second and the next ones enter as an index, as in a_{2k}. In programming, the index is not explicitly used in the variable, which can be from one to eight characters. In Basic and other languages, there are two fundamental requirements for the variables: we cannot use reserved words nor start with numeric or non-letter characters. The first symbol of the variable must always be a letter, from a to z. Basic is not sensitive to type (uppercase or lowercase), so that **a** and A are the same variable, this being another ease of language, because in others, such as C++, **a** and A are distinct variables.

Data. In the abve program, which calculates average of two numbers, we can leave open the value of these numbers, so that the future user of our application can enter his own data. Let us do this, for example, with a second program.

Given two integer values of legs, we will construct a program that gives the value of the hypotenuse. A triangle has a guaranteed existence when the sum of the two smaller sides exceeds the larger side, but we do not need to test this here, because it is precisely the larger side that will be calculated, the hypotenuse, which, by the Pythagorean Theorem, has as its square the sum of the square of the legs. Its value is, therefore, the positive square root of this sum.

The program will be:

```
Function Hypoten(m, p) As Double
    Rem Sample Program 2
    Dim b, c As Integer
    Dim to As Double
    b = m: c = p:   Rem Cathetus
    a = sqr (b ^ 2 + c ^ 2)
    Hypoten = a
End Function
```

For the statements to be strictly completed, the first line above would have to be written as Function Hypoten(m As Integer, p As Integer) As Double, that is, the variables within the argument would have to be declared as well. Since the variables that replace them in the fourth row are declared as integers, Basic can dispense with the statement of **m** and **p**, with the user knowing that if he writes non-integer rational values, only the integer parts in the execution will be considered.

When the user calls this function in some cell of the worksheet, it is not enough to just write the symbol "=" and the name of the function. It is now necessary to provide in the parentheses the values for the cathets, which, as stated in the program, must be integers.

Note: In the code window, the symbols for operation and number writing are in English. In the spreadsheet, if it is translated into Spanish, Portuguese, or another Latin Language, everything is written according to the rules of the referred language. Thus, the user would write in a spreadsheet in English =Hipoten(3, 4), but in Portuguese, that uses comma to separate decimal part, the writing will be =Hipoten(3; 4). The result, hypotenuse of the triangle with legs 3 and 4, should be 5. If another thing appears, the program is typed wrong, or some other error occurred.

Let us try a more enriched example, joining alphanumeric variable (String) and numeric variables. It is to calculate the area of a triangle, by the Heron's formula, given the three sides, typed in ascending order.

In this program, we will first test if the triangle exists, that is, if with the three sides typed by the user the triangle is constructible. It will look like this:

```
Function Triangle(x, y, z) As Variant
    Rem Sample Program 3
    Dim area, a, b, c, s As Single
    Dim resp As String
    a = x: b = y: c = z
    If c < a + b Then
        s = (a + b + c) / 2
        area = (s - a) * (s - b) * (s - c))
        resp = area
    Else
        resp = "Not-constructible-triangle"
    End If
    Triangle = resp
End Function
```

Conditional. The novelty here was the introduction of the reserved word *If*, which forms the *If... Then... Else... End If* statement. Can be used only with If... Then, or with If... Then... Else. The statement with If tests a condition, for which it is called conditional execution: If sentence A, then sentence B, else sentence C. In this example, if the greater side **c** is less than the sum a + b, then the triangle exists and the calculations are made. Otherwise, the answer is that the triangle is not constructible, because the three sides do not close.

In the three above programs, the user saw how we can calculate value through a formula and get the result in a cell of the corresponding spreadsheet (when opening the code window, it is associated with a spreadsheet, indicated in the menu that appears on the left). The first one calculates the arithmetic mean of two numbers. The second, finds the hypotenuse given the legs, while the third uses the Heron's formula to calculate the area of a triangle.

The dear reader is now able to elaborate a myriad of programs that use formulas to obtain values.

9

Exercises:

0.01) In a program assign different values to variables **a** and **b** and give as a result the value obtained in the formula $(a+b)/(a-b)$. The argument must be empty, that is, if the program is called Calculate, it will be called in the worksheet as =Calculate( ).

0.02) Create a program that converts a given measure in degrees Fahrenheit, typed in the spreadsheet, as an argument, to temperature in Celsius (for such a thing, isolate C in the formula $C/5 = (F-32)/9$).

0.03) Make a program that gives the value of the discriminant (delta, or b^2-4ac) of a second-degree equation, of coefficients **a**, **b**, and **c** provided in the spreadsheet.

0.04) Develop a program in which the user provides in the spreadsheet the values of C, **r** and **t** (capital, interest rate and number of months) and has as a result the application amount, by the compound interest formula, $A = C.(1+r)^t$. For example, if the user types within the parentheses 5000; 2; 11, the second value, which is 2%, will be divided by 100 in the program, so that in the formula is 0.02. He has applied 5000 at this rate and wants to know what the amount will be after 11 months.

0.05) Program a national income function (GDP), according to Keynes's formula, $Y = C + I + G + X-M$ (consumption plus investment plus government spending plus exports minus imports). The user must give the values of these five variables and get the product, or income, Y.

0.06) Develop a function that gives the number of diagonals (**d**) of a convex polygon, given the number of sides (**n**), remembering that the formula is $d = n.(n-3)/2$.

0.07) Express a function that calculates the volume of a right-rectangular prism given its dimensions, i.e., width, length and height **a**, **b** and **c**. Formula: $V = a.b.c$.

0.08) Assemble a program that gives the pressure of a gas, given number of moles, temperature, in Kelvin, and volume, in liters, using the Clapeyron equation, $p = nRT/V$. The constant R, as known, is 0.082 atm.L/(mol.K).

0.09) Find, in a function, the result **r** given the intensities **a** and **b** of two vectors and the angle **m** between them, remembering that to find the resultant it is enough to extract the square root of the second member of $r^2 = a^2 + b^2 - 2.a.b.\cos(m)$.

Chapter 1 Overview

Situating. The Excel spreadsheet is part of the MS-Office suite, Windows. Other spreadsheets can be loaded in Windows, and other operating systems have their own spreadsheets.

The most widespread operating systems for PC today are:
* Windows
* Unix
* Linux
* Solaris
* FreeBSD
* OS X
* BeOS
* Plan 9
* Unix

For mobile devices (mobile phones and tablets), the most popular operating systems are iOS, Android, BlackBerry OS, Windows Phone, Firefox OS and Palm OS, among others.

Machine. Computers currently come in a variety of formats. The most robust, in size, remains the mainframe, which is usually arranged in one or more rooms, next to its peripherals. Next comes the PC, personal computer, the desktop microcomputer, developed by IBM. It consists of a case, a box containing the CPU (Central Processing Unit), the screen - which was once a tube television and is now a liquid crystal display - and peripherals such as printer, scanner, keyboard, speakers, external HD, etc. The CD-DVD player is peripheral, but usually comes embedded in the CPU case, which contains the processor, memory cards, sound card, video card, communication ports (printer and internet), the cooling fan and the internal HD. In descending order of size, what comes next is the laptop, or portable computer. Because of the ease of use, and because it is based on the same technical design, although with a different format, its quantity exceeded that of desktop computers. With a smaller size, keeping the format of the laptop, the netbook was launched in the early years of the 21ˢᵗ century, with CPU differing from the laptop because it does not contain a CD-DVD player, given the lack of space. Further down the scale of size, the next computer is the tablet, a generalization of the Apple Ipad, which, in turn, is a device inspired by Amazon's Kindle reader. Finally, one has the smallest of all, which is the smartphone, generic of the Apple Iphone, miniaturization of the Ipad, developed to be a cell phone with the basic facilities of a computer.

In a computer, each type of peripheral has its interface, a device that connects the part to the CPU, translating between the two. Memory, the most important part of the computer after the processor, is divided into three types, according to their use: ROM (*read only memory*), RAM (*random access memory*) and auxiliary memory, which are the storage, operating and query devices, such as internal HD, external HD, flash-drive, floppy disk and cloud storage devices, that is, from the internet.

In computing, the physical machine composes the hardware area, while the intelligence sector, that is, programming, composes the software area. The elements of computing play the role of input (input devices) or output (output devices).

History. Many seek to discover who was the father of the computer, as if there had been an individual who had created the device at once. What one has, in fact, is a succession of gains in the development of what is understood by computing in the present times. The first big step, in the physical part of the business, was given by Blaise Pascal (1623-1662), with a machine driven by crank. So we can highlight these steps:
* Adding machine (Pascal) - 1642
* Multiplication Machine (Leibniz) - 1673
* Book *Mathematical Analysis of Logic* (George Boole) - 1848
* Analytical Machine (unconcluded - Charles Babbage) - 1837
* Coded Programming (Ada Byron) - 1842
* Pierced Card Loom (Joseph Marie Jacquard) - 1804
* Card Reader (Herman Hollerith) - 1880

* Logical gates (Charles Sanders Peirce) - 1902
* Information Theory (Claude Shannon) - 1938
* Z3 binary computer (Konrad Zuse) - 1941
* IBM Mark I Decimal Machine (Howard Aiken) - 1944
* ENIAC binary computer (John Von Neumann) - 1946
* A-Zero Language (Grace Murray Hopper) - 1951
* UNIVAC I market computer (J. Mauchly, P. Eckert) - 1951
* Arpanet or US Army Email - 1969
* Altair Microcomputer - 1975
* IBM-PC Microcomputer with HD - 1982
* Internet or World Wide Web (Tim Berners Lee) - 1989
(ENIAC: Electronic Numerical Integrator and Calculator.
UNIVAC: Universal Automatic Calculator.)

Operational. An operating system (OS) is a set of programs that manages the hardware (physical machine), establishing its interaction with any program (software), or application, that is used in the computer.

Microsoft's Windows, still the most widely used operating system on PCs, came as a parallel development to MS-DOS from 1981, when it was adopted by the IBM-PC machines, which IBM traded with Microsoft, a beginner enterprise created by Bill Gates. In 1985, Microsoft introduced Windows 1.0, which was a graphical (windowed) interface that the user called on the computer screen from the command line of the MS-DOS operating system. Ten years later Microsoft released Windows-95, which opened directly on the screen as an operating system, without the need to first open up MS-DOS.

Some programs are considered essential for use on the PC nowadays. Among them are:
* Browser (I. Explorer, Google Chrome, Mozilla Firefox,...)
* Antivirus (AVG, Avira, Avast,...)
* Uninstaller (Revo Uninstaller, IObit Unistaller,...)
* Communication (Facebook Messenger, Skype,...)
* Play-video (Windows Media Player, VLC Media Player,...)
* Office (MS-Office, OpenOffice, Google G, LibreOffice,...)

In the Office suite we find the spreadsheets, of which the most used today are as follows:

* Excel - from Microsoft's MS-Office suite
* IBM-Lotus 1-2-3 - from IBM's SmartSuite
* StarOffice Calc - from Sun's StarOffice suite
* Four Pro - Corel's WordPerfect suite
* KSpread - from the Koffice Linux suite
* OpenCalc - from the OpenOffice suite

Excel Visual Basic (Excel VBA) is another of the features that this spreadsheet from Microsoft presents for use by its customers. If the reader does not yet know how to program in any of the other languages and learns to make programs in the Excel development environment, he will be able to quickly master the programming mechanisms in other languages, starting with those in the Basic family such as QBasic, QuickBasic and Visual Basic, and he is recommended, if he wants to deepen into the subject, to study languages like C++ and Pascal, before trying to become expert in programming by object, that is, programming for windows, such as Visual Basic and Visual C++.

In the evolution of programming languages hundreds of different codes appeared, some as modifications within well known families, others as independent creations. The most important languages in the human history are:

* Lambda Calculus (1936)
* Plankalkül (1946)
* Short Code (1949)
* Assembly (1950)
* A-zero (1951)
* Fortran (1957)
* Algol (1958)
* Cobol (1960)
* Basic (1964)
* Logo (1967)
* Pascal (1970)

* C (1972)
* Ada (1979)
* Modula-2 (1981)
* Python (1991)
* Visual Basic (1991)
* Visual C++ (1993)
* Java (1995)
* Android SDK (2009)

From the A-zero language, by Professor Grace Murray Hopper, scientists developed the languages that use words of human communication, which are called high-level languages, as opposed to previous ones, with specific codes, called machine languages.

Iteration. With the If command we saw above, the computer appears as a single machine, breaking with all the machines that preceded it, because it can make decisions. For example, if such an action occurred, shut down the machine.

In order for this decision-making ability to be complete, programming languages have developed the *For* (or equivalent) command, which allows the repetition of an action for a fixed number of times, or until a given condition determines the stop. In Basic, what we have is the so-called *For-Next* loop.

For example, we want a program that calculates the sum of the series $a_n = 3n-4$, from the first term ($n = 1$) to the thirtieth. Substituting **n** for 1, 2, 3, etc., we see that the program will add $(-1) + (2) + (5) +... + (86)$. The program will look like this:

```
Function Series1( ) As Integer
    Rem Sample Program 4
    Dim n, s As Integer
    s = 0
    For n = 1 to 30
        s = s + 3*n - 4
    Next n
```

```
    Series1 = s
End Function
```

Checking. To manually check the progress of the execution, it is customary to set up a table with the variables and to calculate at each step the value that each one must have. This is usually done when something did not go as planned. To test the above program, we created the table with the variables **n** and **s**. Below these we will write the value obtained in each iteration. Ignoring the initialization value of **s**, which is before and received zero value, in the first row, under both, the values are 1 and -1, since s = 0 + 3*(1)-4. In the next line, n = 2 and s = -1 + 3*(2)-4, which gives -1 + 6-4, i.e., -5 + 6 = 1. When n = 3, we have s = 6, and the account here is left to the reader. Obviously, we do not need to calculate the values in the hand up to n = 30, because we can change the program for test effect, putting, for example, 4, instead of 30. If the result in Excel is not what our manual account accuses (s = 14) then there is a typo or design error in the code, and the user will have to identify it to make the correction.

A second example shows the use of the For-Next loop to sum a series from a user-provided number in the worksheet as the argument of the function. We know that the sum of the sequence values of the odd natural integers gives the square of the quantity of numbers. For example, 1 + 3 + 5 gives 9, which is the square of the quantity 3. If we add four numbers, 1 + 3 + 5 + 7, we will have 16, which is the square of 4 (we add the first four numbers in the series). So in our program, the user provides a positive integer and the program, which does not know this property of the square of the quantity, will make the sum of the odd ones from 1 to the given value if it is odd. If the data is an even number, it will add up to the previous value, n-1. Numbers can be summed in both ascending and descending order, so we will use the descending sequence, unlike in the previous example program.

17

```
Function Series2(n As Integer) As Integer
        Rem Sample Program 5
        Dim i, k, s As Integer
        k = n: s = 0
        r = k Mod 2
        If r = 0 Then k = k-1
        For i = k To 1 Step -1
            s = s + i
        Next
        Series2 = s
End Function
```

A novelty in the above program is the *Mod* operator, also called **p** Mod **n**. It was created by Carl Friedrich Gauss in the so-called congruences module **n**, and serves to provide the remainder of the division of a number **p** by a divisor **n**. Also the *Step* add-in appeared, inside the For command. It has the same meaning as the step of the Arithmetic Progression. Since in this program we decided that the progression would be decreasing, the step is not 1, which would not require the use of the word Step, but -1; so we have to warn the machine about it.

Flowchart. There are still programmers who draw the flowchart of the codes they produce as a means of verifying visually whether paths and deviations are consistent, that is, whether the program is structured, because a *flowchart* or flow diagram showing crosslines, for example, it may even work in an interpreter, but will present problems in a compiler. An interpreter just runs the program, step by step, and shows the result, whereas a compiler creates an executable version of the code, generating a new file with an extension of type Exe, Com, etc. Before compilation, and as a program to be interpreted, the code is saved in a file whose extension usually refers to the name of the programming environment. For Basic, Bas; for C++, Cpp; for Java, Java; and so on.

A typical flowchart is the one drawn below, made for the Sample Program 5.

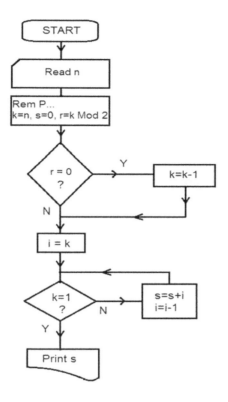

Assignment. Here is a quick discussion on using the equality symbol ("=") in programming. In the expressions k = k-1 and s = s+i, we use the symbol in a way that perverts the traditional algebra. This is because we do not use indices in the variables, once in this second sentence, for example, the meaning is: $s_n = s_v + i$, that is, the new value (**n**) of **s** is equal to the old value (**v**) + i. These indices are, therefore, implied. Because they are not explicit, some languages, such as Pascal, use a modified equality symbol, meaning "attribution". It is written as ":=". In a := b the sense is that to the variable **a**, to the left, the value that was in **b** is assigned.

In the early versions of Basic, the verb Let was used before the assignment, even with the equal sign. Instead of writing s = s+i, we put Let s = s+i. Over time, this word Let was being abandoned.

An alternative to the For-Next loop, which presents even greater possibilities, is the *While-Loop*, or *While-Do* loop. The vast majority of programs with For can be written with While, and vice versa, but there are cases where While makes the service more space-saving and time-consuming.

The processing time, in programming, by the way, is counted via the number of steps. If a program comes to a result using five thousand steps, including steps within iterations, and another reaches the same point using only two thousand steps, this second one must be taken as the most efficient.

At the beginning of programming practice the languages used to present the GOTO command (go to), which worked in place of the For and the While. The problem is that, using GOTO, the program is often no longer structured, that is, it does not present an appropriate flow for compilation.

An example is to make the sum of the squares of the positive integers even while the result is less than or equal to, say, 400.

```
Function Ssquare1( ) As Integer
    Dim k, t As Integer
    k = 0: t = 0
    Back: k = k + 2: t = t + k ^ 2
    If t < 400 Then GO TO Back
    Square1 = t
End Function
```

Surely the programmer can try out the above program, but then he might want to write it in a definitive, and modern way, using For-Next or While-Do. It will look like this:

```
Function Square2( ) As Integer
      Rem Sample Program 6
      Dim k, t As Integer
      k = 0: t = 0
      While t = 400
         k = k + 2: t = t + k ^ 2
      Do
      Square2 = t
End Function
```

From the fourth line, instead of While... Do, we could have used the alternative way of While, doing: Do While t <= 400: k = k + 2: t = t + k ^ 2: Loop.

Stopping. At this point we have to alert to the problem of the stop condition in the programs. If, inadvertently, using For or While the developer leaves the code without a mechanism that causes it to terminate the execution at a certain point, then the program goes into "loop." The user will not need to turn off the machine to stop the program. In Excel VBA, simply press the Ctrl + Break combination on the keyboard. If one wants the computer to resume from the point where it stopped, he simply presses F5. To make the program show step by step, the key used is F8.

Using While, let us develop a very useful example program that provides an important technique for using variables. This is to create the function that gives the Highest Common Factor of two numbers.

```
Function Hcf(n, p) As Integer
      Rem Sample Program 7
      Dim k, m, p, d, r As Integer
      m = n: d = p: k = 0
      If m < d Then
         k = m: m = d: d = k
      End If
      r = 1
```

21

```
    Do While r > 0
        r = m Mod d
        m = d: d = r
    Loop
    Hcf = m
End Function
```

After we have stored the values given in variables **m** and **d**, which will be, respectively, dividend and divisor in the next process, we must verify if the major-minor hierarchy is satisfied. If the given numbers are, for example, 5 and 20, we will not find the HCF dividing 5 by 20, but doing the opposite, 20 by 5. Then the test starting at line 5 will solve the situation. If m < d, we change the values. How can we do this in a program? We know that if we assign the value of **d** to **m**, we will have two variables of the same value, and we will lose the value that was stored in **m** previously.

There is a library function, Swap, that plays this role. But let us not use it now, because not all programming languages have it. Let us do explicitly what is inside it. The artifice is as follows: we first store the value that was in **m** in a third variable, **k**, which serves only for this purpose. Then we launch in **m** the value that was in **d**. Yes, the old value of **m** was destroyed in it, but not lost, because it is in **k**. Now just assign the new value of **k** to the variable **d**. That is what is written on line 6.

In line 8 we initialize a variable, **r**, to have the role of the remainder of the division. Finally, in line 9 we begin to calculate the HCF. While the remainder **r** is greater than 0, we calculate the value of the remainder of the division of **m** by **d** by storing it in **r**. Then we assign the value of **d** to **m** and the value of **r** to **d**, resuming the cycle. When this remainder is 0, and in this case the divisor is being 1 or some value greater than this, with exact division, then the cycle ends and the last value of **d**, which was for **m**, is posted in Hcf.

Exercises

1.01) Using For, write a program that sums the series $a_n = 2n+3$, until the **n** position is 25, that is, up to the twenty-fifth term, from n = 1.

1.02) Make a program, using For, that gives the sum of the multiples less than a given value typed by the user.

1.03) Using While, create a program that sums the Arithmetic Progression, in descending order, with the step of -1, from the number 1000 to a value given by the user. The program must test at first whether the given value is less than or equal to 1000, so that if it is greater than 1000, drop the result to 0.

1.04) Create a program, using While, that traverses the multiples of 3, from zero, and results in their sum as long as they are less than 40.

Chapter 2 Alphanumeric functions

Writing. In the first decades of computing, communication between human and machine was done through numbers. The typewriter was one thing, the computer was quite another, which served to compute, that is, to make calculations, or accounts.

Between 1949 and 1951, scientists created programming languages that allowed the entry of letters into the machine, not just codes directly representing numbers. These letters, as they are today, are immediately transformed into numbers within the computer, and from the context presented to it, it separates the number that represents letter from the number that means number itself (in Ancient Greece, numbers were represented with letters of the alphabet and, for the reader to distinguish who was one and who was another, numerical values were preceded by an apostrophe).

Later, variables, which, as we know, are letters or set of letters, come to represent not only numerical value, but also alphanumeric value, that is, words. The variable X, once it is set to Integer, Single, Double, or any other code that tells the machine that it is numeric, will receive a value that will be processed as a number. If, on the other hand, the programmer declares it as String, the content that will be stored in it will be a letter or a word, even if it is a number. If X is String and receives the value 5, it is "understood" as "5", that is, the character "5", not the numeric value that is half the value of 10. The variable can receive, for example, a car plate: X = "2CKP534".

Functions. In the spreadsheet environment Excel has many numeric and logical functions. In the programming environment, Excel VBA includes these functions and also the alphanumeric functions, stored there so that the developer can use it for the most varied possible purposes.

The most used alphanumeric functions of Basic are those that are used to manipulate strings. They are Left\$, Right\$, Mid\$ and Chr\$, used according to the structures:

24

Left$(X$, n)
Right$(X$, m)
Mid$(X$, i, k) and
Chr$(n)

The dollar sign, $, at the end of the X variable and at the end of the function names, represents one more of Basic's malleability. Variable, or function, with this symbol means that it is alphanumeric. If the user declared previously the variable as String, the dollar sign is expendable. In the case of functions, as they are already in the Excel VBA library, whether or not one writes the dollar sign it does not matter..

Given that we will declare the variables to use, we can write the above expressions as Left(X, n), Right(X, m), Mid(X, i, k) and Chr(n). This is much simpler. When we write Y = Left(X, n) we are saying that Y will store the first **n** characters, or the **n** characters on the left, of the contents of the variable X. Thus, if X = "Cambraia" and n = 3, Y =Left(X, n) will result in Y = "Cam".

For the same alphanumeric value of X, if we write W = Right (X, 4), the resulting value will be W = "raia", the four letters to the right.

The Mid(X, i, k) function gives **k** characters of X starting from the i-th position. Continuing with X = "Cambraia", the expression Z = Mid(X, 2, 6) results, therefore, in Z = "ambrai".

The Chr function, of Character, results in the letter, or any other character whose number in the ASCII code is **n** (ASCII: *American Society Code for International Interchange*). For example, the uppercase letter B is 66, so V = Chr(66) results in V = "B". If we do V = Chr(65), the result is V = "A".

There are also some functions of numerical result with a necessarily alphanumeric argument. They are: Val, Len, Asc and Instr.

The Val function transforms into numeric content the value of a variable previously considered as alphanumeric. If X = "5", then y = Val(X) causes the numerical variable **y** to be 5.

Len, which comes from Length, gives the size of the alphanumeric content. Thus, k = Len("Massachussets") assigns the value 13 to the variable **k**. Asc gives the number in the ASCII code corresponding to the contents of the variable in the argument. Thus, n = Asc("A") results in n = 65, while p = Asc ("a") causes the value of **p** to be 97.

From In String comes the Instr( ) function. In m = Instr(n, X, A), the value of **m** will be the position of the first character, or the first block, represented by A within the expression X, starting the search for position **n**. If **n** is omitted, the search will be done from the first character. If X = "Brazilians communicate", the value of **p** in p = Instr(X, "i") will be 5, because the first "i" is in the fifth position.

An example program will be an application that receives a word entered by the user in the worksheet as the function's argument, and results in another word formed by the even-numbered characters within the given word. So, if the word is "Millennium", the result is "ilnim".

```
Function Skipping(p As String) As String
    Rem Sample Program 8
    Dim Wo, Med As String
    Dim i, n As Integer
    Wo = p: n = Len(Wo): Med = ""
    For i = 2 To n Step 2
       Med = Med + Mid(Wo, i, 1)
    Next i
    Skipping = Med
End Function
```

After saving the program, if the user type in any cell of the worksheet related to the expression =Skipping("Mariette"), for example, the result should be "aite".

This symbol "+" between Me and Mid can be replaced by "&", which has the meaning of addition, or concatenation, in alphanumeric values.

Let us make now a program that, using the Left, Mid and Right functions, select the letters to the left, middle, and end of a

26

given word, forming a new word. If the quantity is even number, the Mid function must pick up the two middle letters, since there will be no "middle".

```
Function Alphaomeg(s As String) As String
     Rem Sample Program 9
     Dim p, new As String
     Dim k, m, t As Integer
     p = s: t = Len (p)
     If t Mod 2 = 0 Then: Rem Even Number
        m = t / 2
        j = 2
     Else
        m = Int(t/2) +1
        j = 1
     End If
     new = Left(p, 1) & Mid(p, m, j) & Right(p, 1)
     Alphaomeg = new
End Function
```

In the fourth line after If, we introduce the numerical function of library *Int*. This is the floor function, or integer function, which gives the largest integer value before the fractional value that comes in the argument. If the argument is 5/2, or 2.5, the result is the integer 2. If the argument is already integer, the result is the value of the same argument. Thus, Int(4.9) = 4 and Int(4) = 4. It is a very useful function in programming. Attention: Int(-5,2) = -6, because if we add -0.2 to -5 we get below -5, not above.

Comparation. The relation operators, <, <=, > and >=, can also be applied to alphanumeric contents. If one word is greater than another, "Marianna" and "Maria", for example, is worth the symbol of ">" to compare them: "Marianna" > "Maria". If we compare characters, the order is given by the position in the ASCII code: "B" < "b" and "A" < "B", for example.

Exercises.

2.01) Create a program that assigns words to different alphanumeric variables, for example "Visit", "the", "beaches" and "of Rio.", and concatenate these words in a sentence, using "+" or "&", with this sentence bein the result of the function.

2.02) Make a program that receives a word, typed as a function argument, and return it inverted. For example, by typing "PARIS", get "SIRAP".

2.03) Develop a program that, by getting a capital letter in the function's argument, results in the corresponding lower case letter. Note that the ASCII value of a lowercase letter is 32 above the uppercase code. For example, Asc("A") = 65, while Asc("a") = 97.

2.04) Elaborate a program that receives a word as an argument of the function and results in the second half of that word, if it has an even number of letters; or the second part after the middle letter, if it has an odd number.

2.05) Assemble a function that receives a word as an argument, turns the letters in upper case, if lowercase; make the arithmetic mean of the ASCII code of all of them; take the integer part of that mean and return the uppercase letter that has that average value as an ASCII code.

Chapter 3 Numeric functions

Calculating. Like the Excel spreadsheet environment, the Excel VBA programming environment also has its library of numeric functions. Obviously, the user can create a myriad of own functions, but the fact that the basic mathematical functions are available for use in programming is very practical.

Constants. As the reader knows, the simplest type of function is the constant, followed by the first degree function, the quadratic function, and so on. The constant function is that whose result (y) is always the same, regardless of the value of the argument (x). If we have to multiply a variable x in it, it must be raised to zero, so that the product is always by 1 ($x^0 = 1$, for any x).

Constants are, after all, unvarying numbers which, when they represent rational numbers on a decimal basis, can be written basically in two ways on the computer: the fixed-point constant and the constant in scientific notation, or floating-point constant, also commonly referred to as a ten-power notation.

We can have, for example, the constants 21.475 (or 21,475 in latin languages) and -5.48 (or -5,48). The numbers $3.9*10^{-5}$ and $-1.3*10^{13}$ are written as 3.9E-5 and -1.3E13.

The above constants are written in the same way in other languages. The non-decimal constants, that is, the binary (base 2), the octal (base 8), and the hexadecimal (base 16) constants, have specific notations in Basic, being preceded by &B, &O and &H.

So we can have:

Binary constant: &B10010101

Octal constant: &O350274

Hexadecimal constant: &H52BE2A

Some functions relate to constants. The Csng and Cdbl functions, for example, transform the value that is in the argument into constant of single precision and constant of double precision, respectively.

Besides the function Int, seen above, with similar role we also have the functions Cint and Fix. The first one, Cint, rounds off the number, while the second truncates the numeric value, throwing out what comes after the decimal point.

Mathematics. Also the known elementary mathematical functions are in the Excel VBA library and many other languages.

Among the mathematical functions of numerical argument we have:

$y = Sin(x)$, x in rad

$y = Cos(x)$, x in rad

$y = Tan(x)$, x in rad (tangent)

$y = Atn(x)$, s real (arc-tangent)

$y = Log(x)$, x positive real, base e.

$y = Exp(x)$, real x, base e.

$y = Sqr(x)$, real non-negative x (square root)

$y = Sgn(x)$, real x (signal: $y = 0$, if $x = 0$, $y = |x|/x$, otherwise)

$y = Rnd(x)$, real x (random numbers)

$y = Round(x)$, real x (rounding)

$y = Abs(x)$, real z (absolute value: $y = |x|$)

$y = Int(x)$, x real (whole floor: $y = [x]$)

$y = Fix(x)$, x real (truncation: $y = x- (|x| - [|x|])$)

$y = Cint(x)$, real x (rounding: $y=0$, if $x=0$, $y = [x+|x|/2x]$, others)

$y = Csng(x)$, real x (single: $y = x$, with 6 digits)

$y = Cdec(x)$, real x (converts to Decimal)

$y = Cdbl(x)$, real x (double: $y = x$, with 14 digits)

The following program takes an integer value that the user provides in the worksheet, understood as positive measured in degrees, positive or zero, and transforms it into radians, to then calculate the cosine.

```
Function Cosdegree(n As Integer) As Double
      Rem Sample Program 10
      Dim k As Integer
      Dim x, and As Double
      k = n
      If k > 360 Then k = k Mod (360)
      x = k * 3.141592/180
```

```
            y = Cos(x)
            Cosdegree = y
End Function
```

The reader should note that, in the If line, the program assigns to **k** the value of the first postive determination of the angle. If the supplied angle is, for example, 750°, it takes the rest of the division by 360°, the measurement of the turn in the cycle, which will give 30°. In the next line the value is passed to radians and the cosine is calculated just below.

The next program is to count the number of binary digits (*bits*) of a given value in decimal base, that is, the user types any integer, such as 378, and the program shows how many digits it would have if it were written on base two. As seen above, the Log function of Excel VBA is in neperian base, base *e*. To find the logarithm in base two we have to make the base change: logarithm in the new base is equal to the logarithm of the value in the old base (10) over the logarithm of the new base (2) in the old base (10). What matters is the integer quantity, so we take the value via the Int function.

```
Function Countbin(p As Integer) As Integer
        Rem Sample Program 11
        Dim n, and As Integer
        n = p
        y = Int(Log(n)/Log(2))
        Countbin = y
End Function
```

Recursiveness. The recursive procedure, in which an operation in a sequence is followed by the same operation applied to a lower order term, with the repetition of the action until the initial term is reached, is a useful, economical and widely used method in programming. The following program uses recursion to compute n! (i.e., **n** factorial), which, as we know, is the

31

multiplication of the positive integer **n** by the predecessor, recursively, to the number 1, which is represented in the formula n! = n*(n-1)*(n-2)...*3*2*1. The number 5!, for example, is given by 5! = 5*4*3*2*1, which results in 120. Remember that 0! = 1.

```
Function Factorial(n)
      Rem Sample Program 12
      If n = 0 Then Factorial = 1 Else Factorial = n*Factorial(n - 1)
End Function
```

Exercises.

3.01) Create a program that results in the number of digits of a given integer on a decimal basis. For example, by supplying 48572, the result should be 5. The argument should be declared as Long, not Integer, which contains few digits.

3.02) Elaborate a program that gives the integer part of the square root of a number taken in absolute value. If, for example, the given number is -17, the program uses the absolute value, +17, finds the square root and gives the integer part, which will be 4.

3.03) Make a program that gives the tangent's value of a given null or positive integer angle in degrees, even if it is above 360°.

3.04) Assemble a program that, receiving a nonnegative integer angle, as in the previous one, computes the sine and gives as result its signal, if positive or negative.

Chapter 4 Subroutines

Extending. So far we have been dealing with functions. All programs made use of library functions or create new functions, but always aiming to achieve a result from one or more data provided to the program or generated within it. As the reader has learned in Mathematics, a function has a single image value for each point in its domain. Knowing how to create functions is no small matter, but we need now to expand our range of possibilities, developing programs that can provide diverse results, and that can use more than one Excel spreadsheet cell for their answer. These programs are called subroutines, within the Excel VBA environment.

Procedure. Subroutine, or procedure, in the various programming languages refers to a block of code that is called within a program, usually exerting repetitive role. If the programmer needs to call within a program the value of profit relative to the sale of a given commodity, he can create the subroutine that makes that calculation, give it a name and use it whenever he needs it.

In Excel VBA, the subroutine has the meaning expressed in the previous paragraph, but it also represents something more elastic than a simple function, which can fit within itself functions as well as other subroutines.

Cells. From now on, we can choose in which worksheets and in what set of cells we want to make the results appear. For this we have to write in some line of our program the command Worksheets( ).Range( ).Value =...

The reader should note that the great change of nature between function and subroutine in Excel VBA is that in the first the user chooses any cell and in it writes the name of the function, with the argument, preceded by the symbol "=", while in the subroutine the programmer is the one who previously chooses in which cell, or set of cells, the result will be shown.

The Worksheets object argument is, of course, the name of

the worksheet. If the user did not change the default name, it will be Plan1, Plan2, etc. The Range object argument is the position of the cell, with the information of the column letter and line number. These arguments, both Worksheet and Range, are alphanumeric. The Value element is classified as a property, related to the objects that precede it in the command. If we want, for example, in the "Plan1" worksheet to write the word "Marques" in line 5 of column A, then we have to include this line: Worksheets("Plan1").Range("A5").Value = "Marques".

The meaning of the above expression can be understood as: Cell value A5 of the Plan1 worksheet is equal to "Marques".

Let us make a small program that shows the values of the ASCII code, in two columns, in the worksheet 2 (Plan2) of the spreadsheet environment, in the first of which we bring the numerical sequence, from 1 to 223, and in the second the symbol that the system stores in each number. As in the assignment to Value the variable i is added to 32, the range of variation of the code goes from 33 to 255.

```
Sub Giveascii( )
    Rem Sample Program 13
    Dim n As Integer, i As Variant
    n = 223
    For i = 1 to n
        cel1 = "A" & i
        cel2 = "B" & i
        Worksheets("Plan2").Range(cel1).Value = 32 + i
        Worksheets("Plan2").Range(cel2).Value = Chr(32 + i)
    Next i
End Sub
```

The reader should note that in the first row with Worksheets the value 32 + i results in integer (Integer), while in the second row the value is Chr(32 + i), which is an alphanumeric (String) content. This object-property set works, therefore, as if it were a variable declared as Variant.

34

There is still a detail to distinguish a program that is a function of one that is subroutine. In the function, we write in the worksheet, after the equality symbol, the name and the argument, after the "=" symbol, and right there in the same cell, the result comes. In the case of a subroutine, whose place of presentation of the result is chosen in the program itself, the mode of execution is somewhat different: just click the blue arrow at the top of the programming environment. It is the first of three small blue icons: Run, Pause and Stop. And how does Excel know which program we want to run if we have multiple applications typed in the module window? Now, the focus, the mouse click, must be within the program, between Sub and End Sub.

The following is a program that makes only one call to the Worksheets object, iterated 14 times. He picks up a seven-letter word, already embedded in it, and writes it in column "B" of the spreadsheet by swallowing one end letter at a time, to the halfway, and then returning those letters one by one.

```
Sub Funnel( )
   Rem Sample Program 14
   Dim alf, ce, x As String
   Dim b, m As Variant
   x = "PROJECT"
   For m = 1 to 14
      ce = "B" & m
      If m <8 Then alf = left(x, 8 - m) Else alf = left(x, m - 7)
      Worksheets("Plan3").Range(ce).Value = alf
   Next m
End Sub
```

In the first line after For we construct the contents of the variable ce, letter and number for the set of cells (Range), to get then the contents of Value, which will be the part of the word printed on the indicated line of the worksheet. The If constructs the contents of the variable alf by removing or adding letters in the word as we are before the position m = 8 or after it.

35

Modification: Swap PROJECT with a larger word, also with an odd number of characters, and adapt the following lines in the program.

The next program again explores the case of more than one call to the Worksheets object, using two columns of the worksheet to expose the sequence of the first positive integers and their respective square roots, which will be given in columns C and D of "Plan1".

```
Sub Roots( )
    Rem Sample Program 15
    Dim i As Integer, s As Double, j As Variant
    Dim cel1, cel2 As String
    Worksheets("Plan1").Range("C01").Value = "Number"
    Worksheets("Plan1").Range("D01").Value = "Square Root"
    For i = 1 To 40
        j = i + 2: s = sqr(i)
        cel1 = "$C" & j
        cel2 = "$D" & j
        Worksheets("Plan1").Range(cel1).Value = i
        Worksheets("Plan1").Range(cel2).Value = Format(s, "# 0.00")
    Next i
End Sub
```

The reader notices that the variable **j** is declared as Variant because its value is computed inside the For, in the line next to If, and then added to the alphanumeric contents that make up cel1 and cel2, that is, it changes from integer to alphanumeric of a line to another. The alternative to this would be to assign a variable **k** the alphanumeric of the integer value of **j**, Str(j), which would complicate the code a little more. Because Excel VBA gives us the ease of the Variant declaration, we should use this feature when necessary.

The dollar symbol, $, before C and D in assigning value to variables cel1 and cel2, is not required. When it is preceded by the letter, it serves to fix the position, that is, with $C being written, one has to be sure that the column will always be C, and cannot be changed in the program for B or E or any other.

In the last line of For, the content assigned to Value comes as a formatted number, using the Format function. As in the argument is "#0.00", we are telling the machine that the print should have exactly two places after the decimal point, no matter how many come before.

Modifications: (a) swap 40 in the For line by 140 and #0.00 by #0.000 in the Format argument; (b) change the function Sqr(i) inside the For for Log(i); (c) change the function to Log of base 10 again, that is, for Log(i)/Log(10). The programmer should always save the program before running it.

The next program is very similar to the previous example, except that it calls a function already built by the user, rather than calling a library function. Let us use the Countbin( ) function. If the reader has saved it to another file, copy it now to the file in question, where this example will be typed. Columns C and D, which are already occupied with the result of the previous example will be exchanged for E and F. Note that we introduced the variable **p**, to be used as an argument of the function, since this was the variable applied in the construction of that one, and so is how the subroutine will recognize the call.

```
Sub Countbins( )
  Rem Sample Program 16
  Dim i, k, p As Integer, j As Variant
  Dim celu, celv As String
  Worksheets("Plan1").Range("E01").Value = "Number"
  Worksheets("Plan1").Range("F01").Value = "BinSize"
  For i = 1 To 40
    j = i + 2: p = i: k = Countbin(p)
    celu = "$E" & j
    celv = "$F" & j
    Worksheets("Plan1").Range(celu).Value = i
```

```
        Worksheets("Plan1").Range(celv).Value = k
    Next i
End Sub
```

Modification: Change the Countbin( ) function to another tried-and-tested non-library function (it is said: user-defined function), or create a new function for this purpose.

Random. Among the non-elementary mathematical functions, those most commonly used in programming are *Rnd*, *Int* and *Abs*. The first of these three, which we have not yet used in examples, allows the generation of random numbers, a very useful feature in computing. Rnd comes from Random, and when we write, for example, $y = Rnd(3)$, the machine assigns a rational random value greater than 0 and less than 1. The argument "3" used here is only to fulfill a fantastical role, because any value would serve. In general, we do not use the argument in this function.

There is, however, a disappointment. The result is not perfectly random, because in a next call to the function under the same conditions the value obtained may be the same as before. This means that the machine still does not have the will to create something on its own, even when requested. The reader should not be dismayed or saddened by the situation, as programming languages have incorporated an output that circumvents the problem: randomizing the number generation according to the system clock. Thus, the next time the program activates the Rnd function, at least a fraction of a second has elapsed, and the number generated will be new. In order for the function to be able to use this feature, Basic has the Randomize command, which we use followed by the Timer function, which results in the number of seconds passed since midnight on that day. It is another function that needs no argument, even fanciful. When we write at the beginning of the program, or the block, Randomize Timer, every time we call Rnd in the sequence, the resulting value will come randomized, that is, randomly, although bound to the

```
```

moment.

The program below generates 15 random numbers in the range 0 - 50.

```
Sub Generator( )
    Rem Sample Program 17
    Randomize Timer: 'Randomizer
    Dim a, j As Integer
    Dim cel As String
    Dim k As Variant
    For j = 1 to 15
        k = j + 1
        cel = "$G" & k
        a = Int(51*rnd)
        Worksheets("Plan1").Range(cel).Value = a
    Next j
End Sub
```

The apostrophe, on the third line, after Timer, has the same role as the word Rem. The reader will note that in the argument of the function Int we write 51 multiplied by Rnd for a range of 0 to 50. For the number 50 to be included in the possibilities we would have to go to the next integer, since the value is always multiplied by number less than 1. If we had left 50, even if Rnd was 0.9999, the result inside the parentheses would be 49.99..., which after passing through the Int application would only be 49.

Modifications: change the For for variation from 1 to 6, to generate a game of the Sixth and change the column G in cel to H.

Matrix. Working with arrays in Excel VBA is very easy. If we want to store data in an A matrix of, say, four rows and three columns, we must first allocate space for it, declaring it as a variable with these dimensions, four and three, or, by guarantee, with larger dimensions, something like five and four, even if we only use four and three. If it is of integer values, in a declaration line we have to write Dim A(4, 3) As Integer.

39

More often, however, what we use is the one-dimensional matrix, the simple vector. If we want, for example, to reserve ten positions for the matrix K, of integers, we do: Dim K(10) As Integer. Soon we will see programs that use matrices of this type.

Reading. The interface of the Excel VBA programming environment with the Excel spreadsheet would not be of much value if we could only print results on it and we could not read data. But such a resource is available and has very simple use. The Worksheets object, which is used to print values in the worksheet, through the Value property, is also readable by indicating the location of the cells where the data is located and launching the contents into a variable.

The below program reads an one-dimensional array with 12 integer values and, storing them in another array, places them in ascending order.

```
Sub Sort( )
    Rem Sample Program 18
    'Enter 12 numbers without order in column I of "Plan1"
    Dim n(12), p (12) As Integer
    Ddim celu, cell As Variant
    For i = 1 To 12
        cell = "$I" & i
        n(i) = Worksheets("Plan1").Range(cell).Value
        p(i) = n(i)
    Next i
    For i = 1 To 12
        For j = i To 12
            If p(j) < p(i) Then
                a = p(j): b = p(i): p(i) = a: p(j) = b
            End If
        Next j
    Next i
    For i = 1 To 12
        celu = "$J" & i
        Worksheets("Plan1").Range(celu).Value = p (i)
```

```
        Next i
    End Sub
```

Modification: Change the quantity of numbers to 15 where was 12.

The Excel spreadsheet environment has an operator to transpose array. If we give a 3x2 matrix, for example, it evaluates the dimensions and transposes the vectors, resulting in a 2x3 matrix, that is, a matrix of two rows and three columns. As an example, and exercise, we will create within the programming environment an application to do this transposition. Let us work with a 4x2 matrix, typed in columns L and M of "Plan1". The result should be a 2x4 matrix, under the columns L, M, N and O.

```
Sub Transp( )
    Rem Sample Program 19
    Dim i, j As Integer
    Dim m(4, 2) As Integer
    Dim cel As Variant
    For i = 1 To 4: 'Reading data
        For j = 1 To 2
            If j = 1 Then cel = "$L" & i Else cel = "$M" & i
            m(i, j) = Worksheets("Plan1").Range(cel).Value
        Next j
    Next i
    For i = 1 To 4: 'Cleaning the area
        For j = 1 To 2
            If j = 1 Then cel = "$L" & i Else cel = "$M" & i
            Worksheets("Plan1").Range(cel).Value = ""
        Next j
    Next i
    For i = 1 To 2: 'Assembly of the new matrix
        For j = 1 To 4
            Select Case j
```

```
          Case 1
          cel = "$L" & i
          Case 2
          cel = "$M" & i
          Case 3
          cel = "$N" & i
          Case 4
          cel = "$O" & i
          End Select
          Worksheets("Plan1").Range(cel).Value = m(j, i)
        Next j
      Next i
  End Sub
```

After saving the program, the reader should not forget to enter the 4x2 matrix under the columns L and M. It should be something like:

L M
4 6
2 1
0 7
9 5

Select. The reader certainly noticed two new things in the program. The first is the two-dimensional matrix, $m(i, j)$, as promised above. The use is very simple, just remember that it will be necessary a counter for the column (For i) and another for the line (For j). The second novelty is the *Select Case* command, which is an alternative to If for situations in which conditions unfold in various items. In the initial For loop, in which we read the array, the If statement solved the problem simply because it was only two columns. When we build the transpose, in the last For loop, we have four columns, and then we see that using Case Select is more appropriate.

Modification: Change the program to work with a 4x3 matrix, given in the columns P, Q and R, with the transpose in P, Q, R and S.

Archives. One of the professional activities of the programmer is to create applications that store data in files and access them, for use within the program itself. Files can be created, used and deleted by the application in question.

In the below program we see how you we put together a program that creates a file of friends' phones.

```
Sub Archphon( )
  Rem Sample Program 20
  'Phone file
  Dim n(80), t(80), G(80) As String
  i = 0: n (i) = "&"
  Worksheets("Plan1").Range("I15").Font.Color = RGB(255, 0, 0)
  Worksheets("Plan1").Range("I15").Value = "Name"
  Worksheets("Plan1").Range("J15").Font.Color = RGB(0, 0, 255)
  Worksheets("Plan1").Range("J15").Value = "Phone"
  Do While n (i) <> "": i = i + 1:
    cel1 = "$I" & i + 15
    cel2 = "$J" & i + 15
    n(i) = Worksheets("Plan1").Range(cel1).Value
    t(i) = Worksheets("Plan1").Range(cel2).Value
  Loop
  Open "C:\agenda.dat" For Output As # 1: j = 0
  Do While j < i: j = j + 1
    Print # 1, n(j), t(j)
  Loop
  Close # 1
  i = 0: J 2 = j = 1
  Open "C:\agenda.dat" For Input As # 1
  Do While i <J2: i = i + 1
    Line Input # 1, G(i)
    cel3 = "$K" & i + 16
    Worksheets("Plan1").Range(cel3).Value = G(i)
  Loop
```

```
Close # 1
   'Open \agenda.dat also by Word or Excel.
End Sub
```

As the reader can see in the first Do While loop, the file can contain 15 data lines, that is, 15 names, with their respective phones. Running the first time, without supplying data, the program creates the Name and Phone headers, now colored, using the Font.Color property and the RGB function (Red, Green, Blue). To test, there is no need to fill all 15 rows. By typing in four lines, this will be enough to check the validity of the program. The reader can make, under the columns Name and Phone:

Anne	3748-1523
Maurice	3748-2049
Richard	3788-4107
Roger	3789-5176

What's new here, besides the Font.Color property, were the commands for file handling: *Open, Close, Input, Output, Print#* and *Line Input#*.

The Open command is used to create a file, giving it a name, and at the same time opening it (For Output As) to receive data. This created file is individualized with a number (in our case, # 1). When the data recording job is closed, the file close command, Close, is used, followed by the number assigned to it, # 1. A few lines later, the reader noticed that the Open command was used again. This time, the file, called "C:\agenda.dat", was opened to provide data (For Input As). These are copied from there to print in column K of the worksheet, as it is in assigning value to the variable cel3. The Line Input command, in this last Do While loop, is used to read a whole line in a sequential file. After this copy, the file is closed again with the Close command.

Modifications: (a) Change the number of lines to be read, from 15 to 20; (b) change the color of the header in the lines of Font.Color, changing the values in the RGB function argument, which can receive integer values from 0 to 255.

Formatting. To expand the notions of using formatting, below we have a program that creates a table for values of sine in the first half turn, that is, in the arc that goes from 0 to Pi.

```
Sub Sine( )
    Rem Sample Program 21
    'Calculates sine from zero to pi
    Dim s(11) As Double
    Dim d, F As String, n As Variant
    Dim celu1, celu2 As String
    Worksheets("Plan3").Range("F01").Value = "Angle"
    Worksheets("Plan3").Range("G01").Value = "Sine"
    d = 4*Atn(1)/10
    For n = 1 to 11
        F = (n - 1)*d: s(n) = sin(F)
        F = Format(F, "0. ###"): s(n) = Format(s(n), "0.## 0")
        cellu1 = "$F" & (n + 3)
        celu2 = "$G" & (n + 3)
        Worksheets("Plan3").Range(celu1).Value = F
        Worksheets("Plan3").Range(celu2).Value = s(n)
        Application.StatusBar = "Calculating sine..."
    Next n
    Application.StatusBar = False
End Sub
```

Something that may intrigue the reader is the expression d = 4.Atn(1)/10, but this is nothing more than a way to get a more "precise" value for Pi. The arc whose tangent is 1 is 45°, or Pi/4. Therefore, if we multiply this arc by 4, it will have the value of Pi. The division by 10 is because we are dividing the half turn into 10 pieces, 10 arches. In the next line the first piece is multiplied by 0, by 1, by 2, until completing the half-turn.

As a novelty in the program, in terms of Excel VBA features, the reader noticed the StatusBar property of the Application object. This set causes its contents to be printed on the status bar while the program is running.

The other novelty is a new way of presenting the formatted output, which is to store it in a variable, which in our case was F. Also the sine, in its varied values, was stored in the formatted s( ) array.

Modifications: (a) Refine the number of sine values to its double, that is, by changing the denominator from **d** to 20, without forgetting to change the upper limit of the For to 21 and also the space of the matrix s( ), which cannot be 11 anymore; (b) still with denominator 20 in **d**, try changing the extension of the s( ) matrix and the limit of For, to see that the next sine must be negative (third quadrant).

The difference between filling the format with 0 or with # is that 0 says that the position should actually be filled with the 0 symbol when there is no other digit in place, whereas using # does not imply padding with 0. For example, the number 3.98 formatted as "0.000" will appear as 3.980. Note that a number such as 5.148 if formatted as 0.00, or "#.##" will appear as 5.15 (rounded to the second decimal place).

To make the whole number separated by a comma, every three houses, we write a comma in the formatting, as in "#, #" (in the Latin world, the output is with separation by point).

If we want the number to have an exit preceded by the dollar symbol, $, we write "Currency", surrounded by quotation marks, as in Format(510.05, "Currency"). For the output to be terminated with the percent symbol, %, we write the word "Percent" in the formatting, as in Format(13.7, "Percent"). There is also a standard format, which says that the number will have an output with at least one digit to the left and exactly two digits to the right of the decimal point, and for this we write the word "Standard", as in the example Format(234.452, "Standard ").

We can also format dates. If we write Format(#10/31/2017 15:25:00 PM #, "dddd mm/dd/yy hh: mm: ss"), the output will be Monday 3/10/2017 03:25:00.

We can also transform alphanumeric expressions from lowercase to uppercase, and vice versa, with ">" or "<", and enter characters in the middle of them by the "@" symbol. If we do

Format("peter smith", ">"), the output will be PETER SMITH. And if we write Format("01145931967", "@@@-@@@@-@@@@"), the result will be 011-4593-1967. Pay close attention to typing the quotes in the programming environment, because the default font will have to be Courier, or something close to it, so if we copy something there in Times New Roman font, the interpreter will not be able to read the expression.

Below is a program that tries out various types of formatting.

```
Sub Formats( )
    Rem Sample Program 22
    Dim p As Double
    Dim a, f1, f2, f3, f4, f5, f6 As String
    Randomize Timer
    Worksheets("Plan3").Range("J01").Value = "Formats"
    p = Rnd: a = "Amazonia"
    f1 = Format(p * 100, "0. ####")
    f2 = Format(p * 1000, "Standard")
    f3 = Format(p * 10000, "#, #.00")
    f4 = Format(p * 1000, "Currency")
    f5 = "Mark:" & Format(p * 10, "0.0")
    f6 = Format(a, ">")
    Worksheets("Plan3").Range("J03").Value = f1
    Worksheets("Plan3").Range ("J04").Value = f2
    Worksheets("Plan3").Range ("J05").Value = f3
    Worksheets("Plan3").Range ("J06").Value = f4
    Worksheets("Plan3").Range ("J07").Value = f5
    Worksheets("Plan3").Range ("J07").Value = f5
End Sub
```

Modification: Change the formatting of variable f6, in order to enter some symbols, such as "^", in the middle of the word "Amazonia", of variable a, through the "@" formatting feature.

Exercises.

4.01) Create a subroutine that reads a word written in cell A20 of Plan1 and prints it in cell C18 of the same worksheet.

4.02) Develop a subroutine that reads a word written in cell A20 of Plan1 and prints it inverted, that is, backwards in cell C20 of the same Plan1 (store the characters of the word in an array, and, for that, see sample programs 8, 9 and 18).

4.03) Make a program that generates 10 random notes, from zero to 10, with precision of a decimal, that is, with a place after the dot, printed on cells K01 to K10 of Plan1.

4.04) Assemble a program that generates a base 10 logarithm table for values 1 through 20, with those numbers in column D and the results, their logarithms, in column E of Plan2.

Chapter 5 Logic: Boolean or logical operators

Sentencing. George Boole, in a book published in 1848 with title *Mathematical Analysis of Logic*, studied for the first time the algebraic role of the connectives "and" and "or" in symbolic logic, which in that historical phase was being transformed into mathematical discipline. In his honor the logical operators *And*, *Or*, *Imp* (implication), *Eqv* (equivalence), *Not* (negation), and *Xor* (exclusive Or) are called today Boolean operators.

The Or connective, according to Boole, is used to say "this or that", being able to contemplate both. Already the operator Xor, "or exclusive", means "or this or that", never the two together.

Propositional. From the possibilities of false (F, or 0) or true (T, or 1) results in sentences, with the use of these operators it comes the truth table, in which we do what Boole called "propositional calculus". Quantum Computation, which is being developed these days, promises to use paraconsistent logics, that work with intermediate values between 0 and 1, that is, between False and True, but for now, we continue to use the computational architecture of 1946, binary Aristotelian logic.

The six basic truth tables are shown below.

s	p	sANDp	s	p	sORp	p	NOTp
T	T	T	T	T	T	T	F
T	F	F	T	F	T	F	T
F	T	F	F	T	T		
F	F	F	F	F	F		

s	p	sIMPp	s	p	sEQVp	s	p	sXORp
T	T	T	T	T	T	T	T	F
T	F	F	T	F	F	T	F	T
F	T	F	F	T	F	F	T	T
F	F	T	F	F	T	F	F	F

Let us look at two sentences as an example: s = "Number 5 is prime", p = "Triangle has four sides". We see clearly that **s** is T and **p** is F. We can find such an arrangement in the second line of the truth table. In it we see that sANDp gives F, sORp gives T, NOTp gives T, sIMPp gives F, sEQVp gives F and sXORp gives T.

The following is a small program to illustrate the use of Boolean operators, which in this case are And and Or. The user must provide a positive integer and its successor, for example, 12 and 13. If one does this correctly, a message of hit appears. Otherwise, a mistake message comes.

```
Function Successor(k As Integer, m As Integer) As String
   Rem Sample Program 23
   'Enter a positive integer and its successor
   Dim As As Integer, resul As String
   q = m-k
   If m>k And q<2 Then resul="Right!" Else resul="Wrong!"
   If k <= 0 Or m <= 0 Then resul = "It was positive."
   Successor = resul
End Function
```

Modification: Change the program to decide whether the nines-out of a given integer are an even or odd number; using the Mod operator, once for the divider 9, another for the divider 2.

As not all implementations of Basic, like other languages, have the operators Imp, Xor and Eqv, but only And, Or and Not, the programmer can construct expressions equivalent to them, since it is demonstrated in Mathematical Logic that:
A) sIMPp is equivalent to NOTs OR p.
(Example: A=0 IMP 5>4 equals NOT A=0 OR 5>4.)
B) sEQVp is equivalent to (NOTs OR p)AND(s OR NOTp).
C) sXORp is equivalent to (sORp) AND NOT(sANDp).

50

We can also use the two Laws of De Morgan, laws concerning to denial, by Augustus De Morgan (1806-1871), English mathematician friend of George Boole:

I) NOT(sORp) is equivalent to NOTs AND NOTp.

II) NOT(sANDp) is equivalent to NOTs OR NOTp.

Aristotle. The three basic axioms of Aristotle's logic are in the Von Neumann computer architecture, which we still use today. Taking "n" as abbreviation for "deny", "no", "never", "negation of", etc., and "S" as a sentence, the three axioms are these:

1) nnS is equivalent to S. (Principle of contradiction.)

2) S or nS. (Principle of excluded third party, the exclusive or.)

3) S is equivalent to S. (Principle of identity.)

An example for the Excluded Third, or Excluded Middle, the most controversial of the Aristotelian axioms, which means that or the given sentence is worth or its opposite is worth, may be as follows: making S = "Circumference is round", S or nS stands: or "Circumference is round" or never "Circumference is round". The detail is that this principle is what was actually introduced by Aristotle, since the other two had been used much earlier by Parmenides. Incidentally, the embryo of the excluded third party was also in Parmenides, with his idea of the oneness of the Absolute Being, since if there were more than one, someone would be Non-Being.

Here is a small program to confirm Aristotle's three axioms in the Von Newmann computer.

```
Sub Aristotle( )
  Rem Sample Program 24
  Dim As As Integer, s1, s2, s3 As String
  A = 0
  If Not Not A = 0 Eqv A = 0 Then s1 = "Axiom 1 is worth!"
  If A = 0 Or Not A = 0 Then s2 = "Axiom 2 is worth!"
  If A = 0 Eqv A = 0 Then s3 = "Axiom 3 is worth!"
  Worksheets("Plan1").Range("B05").Value = s1
```

```
    Worksheets("Plan1").Range("B06").Value = s2
    Worksheets("Plan1").Range("B07").Value = s3
End Sub
```

Modification: Just change the sentence, from A = 0 to A = 2 + 3, or something like that, writing in the lines of the If A = 5.

This next program uses the Boolean variable declaration, which has two values, True and False.

```
Sub Boole( )
    Rem Sample Program 25
    Dim Test As Boolean
    Dim m As Integer
    Randomize Time
    m = int(2 * Rnd)
    If m = 0 Then Test = False Else Test = True
    If Test = True Then
      MsgBox "Boolean is 'chic'!"
      Else
      MsgBox "Too bad!"
    End If
End Sub
```

In addition to the Boolean declaration, another novelty in the program was the use of the *MsgBox* function, which, as the name suggests, responds to a message box outside the worksheet in question, as if it were a popup, where the user presents some information that can be deleted next by clicking on the "X" in the upper right corner of it. The argument is always an alphanumeric expression (String), or a String variable, and does not need to be enclosed in parentheses.

Modifications: Change, ad libitum, the messages that are as argument of MsgBox; try to write the If of this block on a single line, like the previous one, thus dispensing with the "End If".

The next program uses the And and Not operators to analyze the value of a student grade that the user types in the worksheet in cell A9, in evaluation system from zero to 10, passing it to red if it is less than 5 , and for blue color, if it is greater than or equal to 5.

```
Sub Marks( )
   Rem Sample Program 26
   Dim mark As Double
   mark = Worksheets ("Plan1") Range ("A9")
   If mark >= 0 And Not mark > 10 Then
      If mark < 5 Then
      Worksheets("Plan1").Range("A9").Font.Color = RGB (255,0,0)
      Worksheets("Plan1").Range("A9").Value = mark
      Worksheets("Plan1").Range("B9").Value = "Failed!"
      Else
      Worksheets("Plan1").Range("A9").Font.Color = RGB (0,0,255)
      Worksheets("Plan1").Range("A9").Value = mark
      Worksheets("Plan1").Range("B9").Value = "Promoted!"
      End If
   End If
End Sub
```

If Excel is translated and adapted to Latin country, with a comma in place of a decimal point, the mark we entered must be commated if it is not an integer value, and the program takes care of converting to dotted notation. So if, for example, the user entered 7,3, the program will work with 7.3, but will return the value with a comma to the worksheet.

The underscore in the two above lines is an information to Excel VBA indicating that the line continues. These lines separated by underscore can therefore be written as one line only.

Nested. The novelty in this program, besides the example of the operator Not, is the use of nested If, one inside the other. We can nest several Ifs, but there is a limit to the processing, because from a certain amount of Ifs the interpreter is lost, being safer to use Select Case instead.

In the line of the operator Not, the reader sees that the mark entered must be non-negative and can not be greater than 10, that is, it must be a note from zero to 10. In the nested If, the program gives a color to the content (the mark to be printed) of the cell, it throws that mark there, red or blue, and in the next cell it warns if the owner of the mark is disapproved or if he was promoted.

Modification: Change the mark from blue to green by changing the position of the number 255 in the second RGB. Note that by also changing the values 0 to slightly higher, the user gets other colors or nuances of the colors he already have.

To close this section, let us make a small program where the Boolean variable is the very function that the code creates.

```
Function Newbool( ) As Boolean
    Rem Sample Program 27
    Dim to As Integer, b As Boolean
    Randomize Timer
    a = Int(2 * Rnd)
    If a = 0 Then b = False Else b = True
    Newbool = b
End Function
```

In the line where the value is assigned to the integer variable **a**, the Rnd function is multiplied to generate values from 0 to 1.999..., and since the result is transformed into an integer, only two possible values remain, 0 and 1.

Modification: Change the Rnd multiplier to 3 or more, to see that the probability of getting False result gets much smaller.

As an exercise for memory, the reader is now invited to remember the meaning of the reserved words used so far. A lot of the words that seem reserved are just library functions, so the reserved words, those that appear in blue in Excel VBA, are in small numbers. The reader should seek to review those he does not remember well. They are: Function, End, Rem, Dim, As, Integer, Double, Single, String, Variant, If, Then, Else, For, To,

Step, Next, Mod, While, Do, Loop, Select, Case, Output, Input, Print, Close, Open, Line Input, Boolean, False, True, And, Or, Not, Eqv, Imp, Xor.

Exercises.

5.01) Make a program, as a function, called Evennumber, such that when the user types an even integer it will result in the String "Hit!", and when he enters odd number it responds: "It's wrong!".

5.02) Create a program, such as a function, such that when the user enters a whole mark less than 5, the response "Disapproved!" will appear, and when the mark is a whole number between 5 and 10, the response is "Approved!" .

5.03) Assemble a program, as a subroutine, that generates integers 0 or 1, randomly, assigning them to two String variables **s** e **p**, as "F" or "T", according to the result is 0 or 1, and print somewhere in the spreadsheet in question these two results followed by the result obtained in the Xor operator. When running, check with the truth table: for example, if **s** is F and **p** is T, the result is T, as in the third row of the table.

5.04) Mount a subroutine that generates a random value and test it to see if it is less than 0.5 or greater or equal to it, and then, in Boolean variable, do print in message box (MsgBox) the expression "Low", if it is less than 0.5, or "High", if between 0.5 and 1.

Chapter 6. Colors at the screen

Coloring. In the various versions of Basic the developer can work with colors, be background colors, be foreground colors, to dye texts and figures. We have already seen how in Excel VBA the programmer can work with colors in texts. We will now see how to color cells and cell blocks so as to get more enjoyable effects in spreadsheets.

When one wants to color a cell, or a set of them, one must use the Interior property in the object referring to the worksheet the user is working with. Next, the Color property, our known, is applied, and a value of the RGB function is assigned with almost 17 million arrangements (256^3), or, alternatively, the ColorIndex property is used, to which we can assign a color value between 0 and 56.

The below program applies the blue color to nine cells, in a rectangle started in cell C1 (Chr(67) = "C"), and then erases the color of cell D2, with ColorIndex value 0, to print a word there .

```
Sub Blue( )
    Rem Sample Program 28
    Dim ascs, k As Integer
    Dim col, lin As Variant
    Dim cel As String
    For k = 1 to 3
        For ascs = 67 To 69
            col = Chr(ascs): lin = k: cel = col & lin
            Worksheets("Plan3").Range(cel).Interior.Color = RGB (0,0,255)
        Next ascs
    Next k
    Worksheets("Plan3").Range("D2").Interior.ColorIndex = 0
    Worksheets("Plan3").Range("D2").Value = "Thanks!"
End Sub
```

Modifications: (a) Change, within the For loop, the Interior.Color property by Interior.ColorIndex, replacing the RGB function with the number 5, which gives blue color; try other numbers then; (b) try to make the word "Thanks!" come out colorful; try to change the word for some other.

Other color features are the Colors property, which, instead of dyeing, provides the color of a particular cell, or a set of cells, and the Border property, which colors only the border of the chosen cell. If we want to dye the four sides of the cell, we use Borders.

The next program paints the edge of cell C5 and further dyes the inside of cell C6 with a random color, then shows a message box with the numeric code of that color.

```
Sub Tinge( )
  Rem Sample Program 29
  Dim k. n. P. As Integer
  Randomize Timer
  k = 1 + Int(56 * Rnd)
  n = Int(256 * Rnd): p = Int(256 * Rnd): q = Int(256 * Rnd)
  Worksheets("Plan3").Range("C5").Border.ColorIndex = k
  Worksheets("Plan3").Range("C6").Interior.Color = RGB (n, p, q)
  MsgBox = Worksheets("Plan3").Range("C6").Interior.ColorIndex
End Sub
```

Because the ColorIndex property has 56 colors, in addition to the number zero, which is colorless, the message box shows these values, which are approximations of the colors of the RGB function.

Modification: The reader can create a variable **m**, constructed in the same way as the variable **k**, to replace the RGB function, remembering that the Color property on the same line has to be replaced by ColorIndex.

Below is a program that uses only the even number colors,

between zero and 56. In a set of cells, in the range L1:N8, it chooses for each one whether it will dye the inside or just the edge. If it is just the border, it types an uppercase letter inside.

```
Sub Fulfill( )
  Rem Sample Program 30
  Dim i, k, m, n As Integer, p, cel As String
  For i = 1 to 8
    For k = 76 to 78
      m = 2 * Int(26 * Rnd): n = Int(2 * Rnd)
      p = Chr (k): cel = p & i
      Worksheets("Plan3").Range(cel).Value = ""
      Worksheets("Plan3").Range(cel).Interior.ColorIndex = 0
      Worksheets("Plan3").Range(cel).Borders.ColorIndex = 0
      If n = 0 Then
      Worksheets("Plan3").Range(cel).Border.ColorIndex = m
      q = 65 + Int(26 * Rnd): r = Chr(q)
      Worksheets("Plan3").Range(cel).Value = r
      Else
      Worksheets("Plan3").Range(cel).Interior.ColorIndex = m
        End If
      Next k
    Next i
End Sub
```

Modifications: (a) Using Font.Color, make the uppercase letter to be printed on the cell come with the same border color; (b) change the color codes from even to odd (this occurs by adding +1 to the value assignment to **m**, or will it be -1? Decide).

Music. Not only of colors Excel lives. The developer can also add music to his works. For doing this, a way is to use the Beep relation, a function that has two arguments for the musical note, which are the frequency, or height, and the duration. This function, however, is not available without the programmer making a prior statement.

58

At the top of the code window, of the module in which he is working, the programmer must write, before any function or subroutine, the following declarative:

Public Declare Function Beep Lib "kernel32" _
(ByVal dwFreq As Long, ByVal dwDuration As Long) _
As long

Remember that these three lines separated by underscore can be written as one only line.

After this provision of the statement at the top of the module, the user can insert into a program a line like this:

Beep 440, 500

This code will play a note, frequency 440, for 500 milliseconds.

The user can also make a program to stay playing music, like the one below.

```
Sub Playing( )
    Rem Sample Program 31
    Dim i, mel As Integer
    Randomize Timer
    For i = 1 to 20
        mel = 100 + 40 * Int(10 * Rnd)
        Beep mel, 330
    Next i
    Beep 440, 1800
End Sub
```

Modifications: Change the range of the For loop from 20 to 40 and also the multiplier of the Rnd function, from 10 to 20.

Exercises.

6.01) Make a program that paints Plan3's K10 to N16 cells in the odd-numbered colors, from 1 to 55, in ascending order.

6.02) Create a program that fills the borders of Plan3's K18 to N18 cells with randomly chosen colors.

6.03) Using for the variables c4, d, e, f, g, a, b and c5, declared as Double, the approximate frequency values c4 = 261.6, d = 293.7, e = 329.6, f = 349.2, g = 392.0, a = 440.0, b = 493.9 and c5 = 523.3, draw up a program that plays these notes randomly, lasting 240 milliseconds, up to the hundredth time. Use Select Case to assign notes from c4 to c5 to a randomly generated m variable (Case 1: m = c4...). After Next, of the 100 notes played, add a final Beep with a c5 note and a duration of 1500 milliseconds. The result should be something like a C major sonata.

Chapter 7. Forms

Fill. In common Visual Basic, out of Excel, as in other languages for object, or object-oriented languages, it is customary to speak of user forms already in the first chapters of the manuals, since we do not have a spreadsheet as a result environment, such as Excel, and the programmer has to create his exit windows from the beginning. Since we are in Excel, this work can stay for the final part of the course, as it happens here.

A form is a rectangle with white space, where the user provides information, to get results, or it can be just an output frame, such as a message box (MsgBox).

Obviously, it is not just about writing a code in the module window and running the program. This is still valid, but the programmer must first open an empty form, on which he will have windows and control buttons.

To do this, we recommend that the reader closes all open programs in Excel. Now in the spreadsheet environment, let us give a name to our file by clicking the File menu and clicking Save As. The suggested name is *VbasForm*. Now we go into the programming environment, Excel VBA, to make our programs. To go to the programming environment, we can click the Developer (or Programmer) menu, and enter Macro - Visual Basic Editor, or simply use the Alt + F11 keyboard shortcut.

There are no open module or form windows. The user then starts by opening an empty form by going to the Insert menu and clicking *UserForm*.

At this point, open the form and, at the same time, the *Toolbox*, with the icon on top (hammer and pliers) highlighted. If this box does not open, the programmer clicks on the form area and, if it still remains hidden, go to the View menu and click on Toolbox. In it the user sees a set of icons, for the controls, starting with the select object set, followed by an **A**, for Label, by an icon with **ab**, for text box (*TextBox*), Combination Box (*ComboBox*), *ListBox*, and so on, passing through the *CommandButton*, perhaps the most important control, and the *Image button*, which allows us to insert a figure in the form.

At the outset, we will create a very simple program, so that the reader will familiarize himself step by step with the new techniques.

If the properties window is not open, the reader should go to the View menu and click "'Properties' window", or simply press the F4 key. On top of it, Alphabetical tab, it is the field for the name of the form, or program. Let us call this first one Dimensioner. The reader should click the field to the right of Name and type Dimensioner. This, however, is not mandatory, and the reader can work with the default name that appears there, but it is important if one wants to make new forms (programs) in the same file.

Let us go back to the form. By double clicking on it, the code window appears, already with a subroutine sketch, with the name Initialize. Our program will basically consist of the scaling of the form, with the Height and Width properties. Within the subroutine we can write, in a line, Dimensioner.Height = 100, and, in the following line, Dimensioner.Width = 100. To save time, VBA allows us to write a generic term, Me, instead of the program name. Our subroutine should look like this:

```
Rem Sample Program 32
Private Sub UserForm_Initialize( )
    Me.Height = 100
    Me.Width = 100
End Sub
```

Still in the code window, select the name Initialize, before the pair of parentheses, and click the Click event on the window at the top of the module, to the right. This should bring up a new subroutine, now named UserForm_Click( ).

Using Private Sub indicates that the code is used only within the class that the user is working with, and cannot be called in other programs. The opposite of this is Public Sub. In the case of

62

functions, it is indifferent to use Private or Public.

In this part of the program, we will create the form's rewriting code, incrementing 20 pixels in each dimension every time the user clicks on it.

```
Private Sub UserForm_Click( )
    Me.Height = Me.Height + 20
    Me.Width = Me.Width + 20
End Sub
```

Let us now make a code that will cause the program to *show* the form when the user runs the project. We type:

```
Private Sub Show_UserForm( )
    Me.Show
End Sub
```

If the Toolbox is now hidden, click once on the form, and it will appear (if the tip of the form window does not appear behind the module window, click Window menu and choose Cascade). Let us put some controls in this form right now.

Click the **A** in the Toolbox, and then click a point on the form, preferably the upper left corner, because the result will be a small frame, 100 pixels by 100 pixels. In the Properties window, further down, to the left, verify that the control's name is as Label1. The reader can keep that name, although it can be changed. Look further down the *Caption* property. To the right of it, change the name to "Click off the button", without quotation marks. Click again on **A** and then the form, just below the label already created. Look for the Caption property of this Label2 and write to the right of it: "before closing".

After the two labels have been created, we will now add a command button. Click the CommandButton icon (it has the shape of an inverted L) from the Toolbox, and then click on the form, just below the second label. Look for the Caption property of it (it is in alphabetical order) in the Properties window and, to the right, write "Close".

The form is ready. If it is difficult to make it appear in the environment, click the name in the tree on the left: Dimensioner. To increase or decrease the size of any of the three controls, click once on it and drag the tip by adjusting it.

It is still necessary to write the code for the command button. Double-click it to bring up the code window with the outline of the subroutine. It should be there with the name CommandButton1_Click( ). Fill in the middle of this subroutine with the Unload command, making it look like this:

```
Private Sub CommandButton1_Click( )
    Unload Me
End Sub
```

Having run the program, to close it simply click on the command button where it says "Close". If something goes wrong, or if the reader prefers, can click the "X" in the upper right corner of the form to exit the program. But before that, try the effect indicated on the labels by clicking inside the form, always outside the "Close" button, to see the frame being resized.

Cleaning. In the second program with form we will see how to clean the control boxes, through a subroutine.

While in the programming environment, open a new form by clicking Forms on the left, and on the Insert menu, clicking UserForm. Let us call it Cleaning.

In the Toolbox click TextBox and click on the top of the form, on its left. Instead of just clicking, the user can drag by scaling the box size. Repeat the procedure with a second TextBox, with a ComboBox, a CheckBox, and an OptionButton.

The next step is to add the Command Button, at the bottom of the form, to the left. Let us call it Clean. Now add another Command Button to the right of the previous one, calling it "Exit". Finally, at the bottom of all the form create a Label, labeled "(Click Date)". Remember that, to name, look for the Caption property in the Properties window.

Now, while in the form, double-click the Clear Command Button to bring up the module window. Between Private Sub

64

CommandButton1_Click( ) and End Sub type the suggested name here for the cleanup subroutine: ClearFor.

Just below End Sub, enter the cleanup subroutine, starting with Private Sub ClearFor( ).

The third subroutine is the closing program. If the user wants, he can go back to the form and double-click on the Exit button, to bring up the module window already with the code sketch. But he can also enter the whole subroutine as below. The last code is to create the message that gives the date and time. After that, just run the program by clicking on the blue arrow at the top. Fill in the boxes with some message and click Clear to see the effect. After doing this a few times, click the date label. Click OK in the message box and then click Exit.

```
Rem Sample Program 33
Private Sub CommandButton1_Click( )
  ClearFor
End Sub
Private Sub ClearFor( )
  TextBox1.Value = ""
  TextBox2.Value = ""
  ComboBox1.Value = ""
  CheckBox1.Value = ""
  OptionButton1.Value = ""
End Sub
Private Sub CommandButton2_Click( )
  Unload Me
End Sub
Private Sub Label1_Click( )
  MsgBox Format (Now( ), "dd / mm / yyyy hh: mm: ss")
End Sub
```

Modifications: (a) Delete, in the code and in the form, the TextBox2 box; (b) Add the Show_UserForm subroutine, as in the previous program, although it is not much needed.

Text. The program below automatically creates a text box, when the user clicks the indicated button, and establishes some of its properties. In the opening we also used, to exemplify, the loading of a Windows image, with the *Picture* property and the *LoadPicture* function.

Open a new form and call it the CreateTextBox. On top of it place a frame for image, after clicking that control in the Toolbox. Create two command buttons at the bottom, one on the left, called Click, another on the right, naming it Close. Click the *Image* control at the beginning of the form to start writing the code as follows.

```
Rem Sample Program 34
Private Sub Image1_Click( )
   Image1.Picture = LoadPicture _
   ("C:\Windows\Web\Wallpaper\Nature\img6.jpg")
End Sub
Private Sub CommandButton1_Click( )
   Dim MyTextBox As MSForms.TextBox
   Set MyTextBox = Controls.Add("Forms.TextBox.1", "MyText")
   With MeuTextBox
      .Width = 80: 'Size
      .Height = 30
      .Left = 80:    'Position
      .Top = 50
      .Font.Name = "Arial":   'Font
      .Font.Size = 11
      .TextAlign = fmTextAlignCenter: 'Alignment
      .ScrollBars = 2
      .MultiLine = True:     'Behavior
      .AutoSize = False
      .SetFocus:      'Focus
   End With
End Sub
Private Sub CommandButton2_Click( )
```

```
Unload Me
End Sub
```

The reader should have noticed a new type of statement, which is one of many programming by object: *MSForms.TextBox*. The MyTextBox object was then declared, since the program will itself create a text box. Next we used the word *Set*, which is used to assign to a variable the reference of an object, which in this case is Controls.Add.

The other novelty is the *With - End With* loop, which is also specific to object-oriented programming and serves to economize the repetition of a given expression. Without the With loop, we would have to repeat on each line the MyTextBox object, such as MyTextBox.Width..., MyTextBox.Height..., etc.

After making all the assignments to the properties of the text box in question, we wrote the command to throw the focus inside it, *SetFocus*, ending the With loop.

When running the program, try filling up the text box with at least three lines. Clean the box by clicking the corresponding command button and repeat the process before clicking "Close".

Modifications: (a) Change the size of the box, with other values for width and height; change the font, from Arial to Courier, with size 13, instead of 11.

Another simple program is one that converts to a decimal value a number given in a text box as hexadecimal. A hexadecimal number, as seen before, starts with &H and is followed by digits 0 through 9 mixed with letters A through F (A being 10 and F being 15, as in &HC8, which is 188).

Open a form (Insert menu) and call it Hexas (under Name in the Properties window). Create a label and then its text box. On the label write (in Caption): "Enter hexadecimal number:". Below the label and the text box create two command buttons, one called Convert and another called Finish.

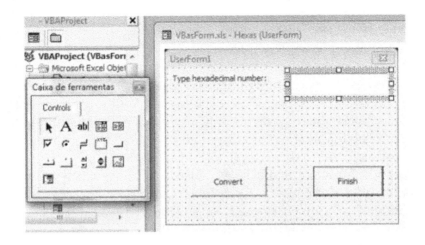

Double click inside the text box to start writing the code, as below.

```
Rem Sample Program 35
Private Sub TextBox1_Change( )
    Dim x As Variant
    x = TextBox1.Value
End Sub
Private Sub CommandButton1_Click( )
    MsgBox "=" & Val (TextBox1.Value)
End Sub
Private Sub CommandButton2_Click( )
    Unload Me
End Sub
```

When the reader runs, by clicking the blue arrow at the top, the focus must be in the text box, and the user must enter a hexadecimal value, starting with &H. For example, &HC8. Click Convert. Try &HFF, &HA11E4, &H777 and other invented values, remembering that the biggest letter to the right of &H is F.

When the reader gets tired, click Finish.

68

Modification: Instead of "=" in MsgBox type something else, like "Okay:".

Interacting. Let us now see how to make the VBA form interact with cells in the worksheet related to it. The following program allows a teacher to type in the form the names of his students and the grades, from zero to 10, of the first and second tests applied, with a result representing the weighted average of the two, with double weight for the second, that is, it counts as two proofs. The user types the header (Name, Test1, Test2, Average) in the row 1 under the columns A, B, C, and D, so that the program will fill that data in the following rows as it receives it on the form.

Create a form, named Students, which has three labels, three text boxes (TextBox), a CommandButton, called Insert, plus a label and a text box, for the result, and finally two command buttons, one called Save, another called Exit. The four labels, in the sequence they appear, are named (Caption property) as Name, Test1, Test2, and Average. Double-click the Insert button to go to the module window and fill in the code.

```
Rem Sample Program 36
Private Sub Insert_Click( )
   Dim Lin As Long, n As Double
   Lin = Worksheets("Plan1").Cells.Find(What: = "*", _
   searchorder: = xLByRows, searchdirection: = xLPrevious, _
   LookIn: = xLValues) .Row + 1
   Worksheets("Plan1").Cells(Lin, 1).Value = _
   Me.TextBox1.Value:      'Copy to Cells
   Worksheets("Plan1").Cells(Lin, 2).Value = _
   Me.TextBox2.Value
   Worksheets("Plan1").Cells(Lin, 3).Value = _
   Me.TextBox3.Value
   n = (Val(TextBox2) + 2 * Val(TextBox3))/3
   TextBox4.Text = n:     'Here goes the average
   Worksheets("Plan1").Cells(Lin, 4).Value = _
```

```
        Format(Me.TextBox4.Value, "# .0")
        Me.TextBox1.Value = "":     'Clear fields
        Me.TextBox2.Value = ""
        Me.TextBox3.Value = ""
        Me.TextBox1.SetFocus
End Sub
Private Sub Save_Click( )
    ActiveWorkbook.Save
End Sub
Private Sub Sair_Click( )
    Unload Me
End Sub
```

When the user clicks the blue arrow to run the program, the Name label will appear, with its text box, the label Test1, with its text box, and so on. An example is to type, from the first box: Peter, Tab key, 3.6, Tab key, 5.9, Tab key. At this point the focus will be on the Insert button. When the user clicka it, the data he enters is inserted into the worksheet and deleted from the form, the average appearing in the worksheet and also in the fourth text box of the form. If everything is right, that average gives 5.1. Of course, other names and their maarks can and should be added before the user clicks the Save and Exit buttons.

Caution: The first line of the header must be typed in the worksheet before the program runs, or an error message will appear.

Remember that, as stated before, the subscript trailing at the end of each line in some parts of the program means that the line continues. VBA interprets this dash as a hyphen, but the programmer can ignore it and pull all of the text onto the same line. In the case of the assignment of Lin, at the beginning, the three lines can be written in one, removing, obviously, the underscore symbols.

The novelty, at the beginning of the program, is the *Find* method, used here to assign value to the Lin variable. Find serves, as the name says, to make the program find values in the worksheet. This "*" is valid as a wildcard, but it could be a specific character, a word or a number, always enclosed in quotation marks.

To print the values in the cells, the code is Worksheets... = Me.TextBox... If we need to do otherwise, bring values from the cells to the form, we write the line upside down: Me.TextBox... = Worksheets...

Modification: Delete the variable **n** by placing Me.TextBox4 in its place, before the averaged formula (the next line, Me.TextBox = n, must then be trimmed).

The next program experiences the use of the For loop with a new complement, *Each*, which serves to search for a given element within a specified group. This group can be a block of cells or a set of data in a user defined group.

Here, we take the block of cells that goes from F1 to J2 in Plan1. We generate values from zero to 10 and print in cells. In the next loop, already using For Each - Next, we look for values greater than or equal to 5 and then color the light blue with each cell that contains them. In the third and last subroutine, before leaving, we created a code to clean these cells, applying the white color - the presence of all colors - on them.

Open a new form by clicking UserForm on the Insert menu, and name it Blue, or some other preferred one. Create four command buttons, called Generate, Mark, Clean, and Exit. By double-clicking the Generate button, the module window appears with the sketch of the first subroutine below, in which the reader will fill the crumb, then do the same with the other three subroutines.

```
Rem Sample Program 37
Private Sub CommandButton1_Click( )
        Dim i, k, m As Integer
        Dim ce As Variant
        Randomize Timer
        For i = 70 To 74:    'Generates ten numbers
```

```
            For k = 1 To 2
            m = Int(11 * Rnd)
            ce = Chr(i) & k
            Worksheets("Plan1").Range(ce).Value = m
        Next k
    Next i
End Sub
Private Sub CommandButton2_Click( )
    Dim n As Variant
    For Each n In [F1: J2]:    'Creates blue borders
        If n.Cells.Value >= 5 Then
            n.Cells.Interior.Color = RGB(200, 255, 255)
        End If
    Next
End Sub
Private Sub CommandButton3_Click( )
    Dim n As Variant
    For Each n In [F1: J2]:      'Does the cleaning
        n.Cells.Interior.Color = RGB(255, 255, 255)
        n.Cells.Value = ""
        n.Cells.Borders.Color = RGB(145, 145, 145)
    Next
End Sub
Private Sub CommandButton4_Click( )
    Unload Me
End Sub
```

Modification: In the third subroutine, of cell clearing, change the For Each - Next command to For - Next, based on the loop used in the first subroutine, the number generation, with Range instead of Cells.

To conclude our series of examples, the next program introduces the use of the user-defined variable declaration, using the Type command, in the Type - End Type loop. It also shows how to use the *KeyDown* event, through which we can press a key specified to get a certain effect. In this example, pressing the Esc key (code 27), when the focus is in the last text box, leads to the program exit.

Open a new form (Insert menu - UserForm) and call it Typecode. It will have four labels, followed by its corresponding four text boxes (TextBox), plus a command button (CommandButton), which will be called Insert, and finally one more label next to another text box.

The first four labels are called Manager, Salary, Customer and Debit, in this order. After the Insert command button, the label that appears below should be labeled "Type Esc:".

Double-click the form to bring up the module window. Delete the subroutine sketch that appears there and select the Declarations section above in the Events window on the left. A menu pops up with only that word, Declarations, and clicking on it causes the focus to go to the code environment, in the module window itself. The Type - End Type loop must be typed before the subroutines and statements with Dim must also be typed in that block. After that, the reader returns to the form to click the command button (called Insert) and thus open the module window again and enter the subroutines.

For the second subroutine, from TextBox5, the reader may want to go back to the form and double-click on this fifth text box, which comes after the label with Esc. If the form does not appear, type the name Typecode on the left. Then a sketch beginning with Private Sub TextBox5_Click( ) will come in the code window. Select the word Click and, in the Events window, click on the KeyDown event to make the change. The VBA is responsible for exposing the statements within parentheses.

```
Rem Sample Program 38
Private Type newtype
    loc1 As String
    loc2 As Integer
End Type
```

73

```
Dim salary As newtype
Dim debit As newtype
Private Sub CommandButton1_Click( )
   Worksheets("Plan1").Range("F4").Value = "Manager"
   Worksheets("Plan1").Range("H4").Value = "Client"
   salario.loc1 = Me.TextBox1.Value
   salary.loc2 = Me.TextBox2.Value
   debito.loc1 = Me.TextBox3.Value
   debito.loc2 = Me.TextBox4.Value
   Worksheets("Plan1").Range("F5").Value = salary.loc1
   Worksheets("Plan1").Range("G5").Value = wage.loc2
   Worksheets("Plan1").Range("H5").Value = debito.loc1
   Worksheets("Plan1").Range("I5").Value = debito.loc2
   Me.TextBox5.SetFocus
End Sub
Private Sub TextBox5_KeyDown (ByVal KeyCode _
   The MSForms.ReturnInteger, _
   ByVal Shift As Integer)
   If KeyCode = 27 Then
      Unload Me
   End If
End Sub
```

When executing the program, the user must enter a person name, after Manager, a value, after Salary, another name, after Client, and another value, after Debit. For example, George, 2000, Lucy, 1800. Clicking Insert now, this data goes to the Plan1 worksheet, under the heading that the program itself has. At this point, the focus was on the last text box. If the user does not want to change George and the other data as experimentation, simply press the Esc key and exit.

As the reader could see, the Type command allows to create a scheme for declaration of variables by the hands of the programmer, but this is not done from scratch. In general, a block is created, defining parts, which enter as properties of the variables to be declared. In our example the created type was called newtype, and the parts are loc1, as String, and loc2, as Integer. Since there were two variables declared in this new definition, salary and debit, they came in separate lines, after Dim. Joining in the same Dim, as in the pre-defined types, would give interpretation problem to VBA.

Back. Enjoy this program to color the form. Go to the Properties window and look in alphabetical order for the *BackColor* property. Clicking the field to the right will bring up a small set, which will indicate colors for the programmer to choose. It is advisable to choose light color so as not to make it difficult to see the names of the labels. As soon as the user runs the program, the form will now appear with background color.

In the TexBox5 subroutine, the key code (KeyCode) is number 27. It is the Esc key code in the VBA. Microsoft provides a table with these values. Start with 1 (left mouse button), 2 (right button), 3 (Cancel button), 4 (middle button), 8 (BackSpace key), 9 (Tab key), 13 (Enter key), 16 (Shift key), 17 (Ctrl key), etc.

Printer. An important note in relation to this or any other program is that if the developer wants to send the result of the worksheet in which he is working for his line printer, simply adds in the program the code:

```
Sub PrintCurrentSheet( )
    ActiveSheetPrintOut
End Sub
```

Modification: Replace the KeyCode value from 27 to 17, Ctrl key, also changing the label on the form, from "Type Esc:" to "Type Ctrl:".

Exercises.

7.01) In a file with a new name, ExerForm, make a program with a form with only two controls: a command button named Hour and another called Exit, so that when the user clicks the Hour button it will be printed in cell B1 of Plan1 the current time (Now).

7.02) Create a program that generates six random numbers for a game of Sixth, from 0 to 50, and shows them in the range A1: A6 of Plan1. The form should have only three controls: a label with the word Sixth, a command button called Generate, and another command button named Exit. The numbers so generated must be stored in a six-term matrix, because they cannot be repeated: if the third value, for example, is equal to the first one, a new number must be generated for the third position.

7.03) Construct a program that evaluates the body mass index of the user, using the formula $I = m/h^2$, **m** being the person's weight in kilograms and **h** the height in meters. In the form two labels should come, each followed by a text box, and two command buttons, one called Insert, another, Exit. In the first label one writes "His mass (kg):" and in the second, "His height (m):". In the subroutine for Insert, the "Index" and "Meaning" headers are printed on cells B3 and C3 of Plan1. In cells B4 and C4, the results of the calculation, i.e., the value of I and the explanatory message, should appear. This will have three possible words: "Lean", if $I<18$; "Obese" if $I>25$; and "Healthy" if I is between 18 and 25.

7.04) Develop a program that receives, in three text boxes, the value of an investment (Capital C), the interest rate (r) per month and the amount (A) that is to be reached, returning, in cell C5 of Plan1, the minimum time required. In cell B5 the word "Time:" should be printed and in cell D5, "months". The compound interest formula, as we know, is $A = C(1 + r)^t$. Then $Log(M)=Log(C(1 + r)^t)$, or $Log(M)=t.Log(C.(1 + r))$, resulting in $t = Log(M)/Log(C.(1 + r))$, and the latter formula is the one which should be used.. Obviously, the labels and the Insert and Exit buttons can not be missing.

7.05) Assemble a program in which the number of faces of a given Plato polyhedron provided by the user in a text box results in the sum of the angles of all faces in cell B9 of Plan1. In cell B7 should be the word Plato, and in B8, the number of faces that the user typed. It is known that the polyhedra of Plato are five: 4 faces (triangular), 6 faces (quadrangular), 8 faces (triangular), 12 faces (pentagonal) and 20 faces (triangular). Thus, the calculation will be given by A = f.(n-2).180 degrees, where A is the sum of the angles, **f** the number of faces and **n** the number of sides of the face (n = 3 in triangular, n = 4 in quadrangular, n = 5 in pentagonal). The code must therefore associate the input **f** value with the number **n** relative to it, with If, Select Case, or another resource.

7.06) Develop a program that calculates the volume V of a sphere whose radius is given in a text box. The buttons are the label with the expression "Radius:", the corresponding text box, and the Insert and Close command buttons. When double-clicking the Insert button, to write the code, the programmer must write instructions to color the borders of the cells of the block F1:H3, of Plan1, and in the middle cell, G2, show the volume value. To get green in the RGB function, the reader places 255 in the middle, which is the G of Green. The formula of the volume is V = (4/3).Pi.r³, and to obtain the Pi with more precision one must do first Pi = 4.Atn(1). Remember that Chr(70) = "F".

7.07) Redo, using form, the program of the exercise 6.06, which creates and plays music, so that it stops only when the user presses the Esc key.

@cacildo
cacildomarques@gmail.com

CHAPTER 1

Introduction

1.1 Context

The way people and companies are communicating and interacting with each other is nowadays very different than decades ago. The standalone mainframe solution in charge of processing information was enhanced with client-server solutions. With the propagation of the internet, quick distribution of information and the interworking among systems started playing an important role. Today, new technologies are enabling companies to virtualize the infrastructure and execute applications using the internet, opening immense possibilities of using software and information technologies "in the cloud".

Cloud computing is considered as the next IT revolution as well as just a hype. The term is not only found in several articles, specialized magazines, books and conferences, but it is also a subject widely discussed in the consulting industry.

Focusing on the industry, cloud computing is gaining importance in many small- and medium-sized companies due to the many benefits in terms of cost savings, faster time to market, mobility and flexibility, among others. Additionally, small- and medium-sized companies using cloud computing services can concentrate on the core business and do not need to invest any effort in setting up and running an own infrastructure and software, which can be replaced with cloud computing solutions.

1.2 Objective and structure

In the scope of this book, cloud computing applications for small- and medium-sized companies are identified as well as the key success factors for adoption of cloud computing services are analyzed based on the empirical investigation performed in scope of this work. The advantages and disadvantages of the different cloud computing service models are also presented including the state-of-the-art research in the area. Additionally, an analysis of the acceptance and current usage of cloud computing in small- and medium-sized businesses is included.

This book is divided into seven chapters:

Chapter 1 gives a short introduction and describes the structure of the document.

Chapter 2 gives basic information about the different software applications used in the industry. Additionally, the term cloud computing is introduced as well as the fundamentals of the success factor's theory. Finally, the forms and characteristics of small- and medium-sized businesses are explained.

Chapter 3 presents the state-of-the-art research in cloud computing and summarizes some studies available in the literature, which focus on the cloud computing model and its implementation in different industry branches. The main results concerning applications and key success factors for adoption of cloud computing services are also presented.

Chapter 4 gives information about the empirical investigation performed within the scope of this book and presents the method used and the survey's sample.

Chapter 5 presents the results of the empirical investigate and analyzes the usage of cloud computing solutions and of the most significant cloud applications for small- and medium-sized businesses.

Chapter 6 outlines the key success factors for adoption of cloud computing services based on the empirical investigation.

Chapter 7 summarizes the analysis of applications and success factors for small- and medium-sized business which were analyzed in this book.

1.3   Methods

Diverse specialized literature and internet websites were used for the preparation of this book. The literature used focuses mainly on cloud computing. The most relevant aspects handled in this literature are:

- The implementation and acceptance of cloud computing in different branches
- The relevance of cloud computing as a new option for companies
- The opportunities and risks of using cloud computing from a corporate point of view
- The strategical approach of cloud computing

The complete literature is available in the library of the Bonn-Rhine-Sieg University of Applied Sciences in Rheinbach and Sankt Augustin, Germany.

Many computer related definitions were taken from business informatics books as well as from experienced and specialized magazines prepared by companies with a broad cloud computing theoretical and practical experience like T-Systems. Cloud computing related definitions were taken also from specialized research companies pioneers in the cloud computing area like Gartner research and Forrester research. The websites from salesforce and the "initiative cloud services made in Germany" were also important sources used in this work.

Some investigations already done in the cloud computing area were used within the scope of this book: the diploma thesis investigating the application of cloud computing in E-business[1] gives a good overview to cloud computing and its application; an empirical investigation performed by the Fraunhofer institute[2] related to the application of cloud computing in the health insurance area provides good information about the practical use of cloud computing. This last study gave good guidelines for the empirical studies done in this work.

Finally, an empirical investigation was done as part of the book, which has been performed in cooperation with the cloud services business unit of Deutsche Telekom. The study consisted of an online survey directed to IT decision makers of small- and medium-sized companies. A total of 613 companies had participated in the survey. The main focus of this survey was the identification of relevant cloud computing applications and the key success factors for the adoption of cloud computing services.

---

[1][11]Möller, Christian: Cloud Computing-Einsatz im E-Business, 2010
[2][23]Weidmann, Monika; Renner, Thomas; Rex, Sascha: Cloud computing in der Versicherungsbranche, 2010

CHAPTER 2

Fundamentals

2.1 Fundamentals of software applications

2.1.1 Definition and characteristics

Software applications[1] are used to perform specific tasks using computer systems. In the last years, software applications gained an important role for facilitating the process of many tasks in parallel and improving the efficiency in the companies.

An application software[2] may consist of a single program, such as a specific invoice program or a chat program. It may be also a collection of programs or software packages that interact closely together to accomplish different tasks, such as spreadsheet or text processing functions. This software is commonly known as software suite. There are also very specific software applications used for engineering, process automation or billing processing. Finally, complex software applications used to coordinate the different aspects of the value chain management play a key role in the companies as the different processes are controlled and managed from a unique application.

2.1.2 Type of software applications

Following sections present the most relevant software applications used in a wide range of industries.

2.1.2.1 Email communication

Email communication software[3] allows to send and receive text messages including also files, audio and video independently of the platform used. It is possible to send email messages to different receiver. It is not required that the users are online in order to receive the messages as they are stored in the exchange servers.

Email software is one of the most used applications in companies.

---

[1]See [44] Webopedia, IT Business Edge: Application software definition,
<http://www.webopedia.com/TERM/A/application.html>
[2]See [37] Open projects software: Software definition,
<http://www.openprojects.org/software-definition.htm>
[3]See [50] Holey, Thomas, et al: Wirtschaftsinformatik, 2007, p. 279

2.1.2.2 Office applications

Office applications[4] refer to applications used to support office activities for word processing, spreadsheet calculations, preparation of presentation slides, graphic arts and database processing. There exist in the market several office applications such as Microsoft office, Lotus Smart Suite, Star Office and Wordperfect Office. The most known application suite is Microsoft Office, which includes Microsoft Word, Excel, PowerPoint and Access. The applications work closely together allowing the easy interaction and object exchange among each other.

2.1.2.3 Project management

Project management applications[5] allow project managers and team members to keep track of any project from its conception to its launch. The software manages all the project related aspects including resource management, budget management, time management, task assignments, quality control, issue reports and documentation management. Project management software provides a centralized view to the whole project and gives more transparency to all involved team members.

2.1.2.4 Team collaboration

Team collaboration software[6] offers proper conditions for the support and coordination of work related tasks within the company or among different companies. Using team collaboration software, project teams can work together to solve common problems and achieve better and faster goals. The team members have the possibility to work in parallel independant of the time and location. Team collaboration software has gained ultimately more importance with the globalization, the internationalization and the geographical distances between teams within the companies.
Team collaboration software combines different office and communication software such as the tools already mentioned in 2.1.2.1 and 2.1.2.2 but also includes project management functions, such as team tasks and time management, shared calendars, real-time joint view of information as well as problem solving processes in teams.

2.1.2.5 Customer relationship management

Customer relationship management software[7] gives the company the tools required to manage customer information. This information is important in order to deliver the customers what they want, provide them the best customer service possible, cross-sell and up-sell more effectively, close deals, understand who the customer is

---

[4]See [43] Holey, Thomas, et al: Wirtschaftsinformatik, 2007, p. 272
[5]See [41] Project management software: Project management software definition,
<http://www.projectmanagementsoftware.com>
[6]See [56] Holey, Thomas, et al: Wirtschaftsinformatik, 2007, p. 281
[7]See [45] Webopedia, IT Business Edge: Customer relationship management software,
<http://www.webopedia.com/TERM/C/CRM.html>

and retain current customers. The customer relationship management software will collect, manage and link the customer information with the goal of optimizing the customer's interaction.

2.1.2.6 Procurement

Procurement software[8] supports the purchase automatization functions in the companies.

All the activities related to create and approve purchase orders, select and order any product or service, receive and match an invoice and pay a bill are handled electronically and can be analyzed separately. The procurement department benefits of the information's centralization as it is possible to see what was ordered, ensure the needed approvals are available and compare current prices to get the best deal for the company.

2.1.2.7 Web development

Web development software[9] relates to software applications used to facilitate the design, implementation and deployment of a company's internet website, applications and web services. This type of software consists of a programming-oriented set of tools for linking web pages to databases and for manipulating other software components. A HTML editor for web development is included generally.

2.1.2.8 Unified messaging

Unified messaging software[10] is used to improve the communication within the company, accelerate and improve the quality of decisions based on real-time information, improve operational effectiveness and reduce travel and expenses cost. The main components of a unified messaging software are instant messaging, fax, email, web conferencing, real-time collaboration, presence and telephony integration.

2.1.2.9 Enterprise resource planning

Enterprise resource planning software[11] allows the companies to use a system of integrated applications to manage the business by integrating all aspects of the company's value chain including development, manufacturing, logistics, sales and marketing. Specifically, the enterprise resource planning software consists of different enterprise software modules, each one is focused on a specific area of the business

---

[8]See [55] Holey, Thomas, et al: Wirtschaftsinformatik, 2007, p. 287
[9]See [40] PC magazine encyclopedia: Web development software,
<http://www.pcmag.com/encyclopedia>
[10]See [34] IBM corporation: Unified communications,
<http://www-142.ibm.com/software/products/us/en/category/SWAAA>
[11]See [46] Webopedia, IT Business Edge: Enterprise Resource Planning software,
<http://www.webopedia.com/TERM/E/ERP.html>

process. The most common modules include those for product planning, material purchasing, inventory control, sales, accounting, marketing, finance and HR. The most important goal of the enterprise resource planning software is to provide one central repository for all information that is shared by all business processes in order to improve the flow of data across the company.

2.1.2.10 Fleet management

Fleet management software[12] is used for managing all the aspects and operations related to a fleet of vehicles operated by a company. Among the main functions of fleet management software are to manage all the processes, tasks and events such as notification of routine maintenance, scheduled maintenance, warranty tracking, work scheduling, depreciation, expense tracking, work order, parts inventory management and operational cost tracking.

2.1.2.11 Human resource

Human resource software[13] is used to support the human resource activities of the companies. The main functions of this software is to provide support in the recruitment process, payroll, time repoint, benefit administration, learning and training management, performance record, scheduling and absence management.

2.2 Fundamentals of cloud computing

2.2.1 Definition and characteristics

The term cloud computing refers to the possibility to execute any kind of process using a server connected to the internet. It is possible to upload and download documents, videos or pictures, which is commonly known as online storage. Cloud computing facilitates as well the execution of computer programs without having them installed at the own machines as the software is executed from supplier's servers connected to internet.

There are many definitions available to describe the term cloud computing. One simple definition[14] refers to cloud computing as the delivery of computing services without owning an own infrastructure.

Other entities define cloud computing as follows:

---

[12]See [51] Wikipedia: Fleet management software,
<http://en.wikipedia.org/wiki/Fleet_management_software>
[13]See [53] Wikipedia: Human resource management system,
<http://en.wikipedia.org/wiki/Human_resource_management_system>
[14]See [10] Metzger, Christian, et al: Cloud computing Chancen und Risiken aus technischer und unternehmerischer Sicht, 2011, p. 2

- NIST[15] defines cloud computing as a model for enabling ubiquitous, convenient, on-demand network access to a shared pool of configurable computing resources (e.g. networks, servers, storage, applications, and services) that can be rapidly provisioned and released with minimal management effort or service provider interaction. This cloud model is composed of five essential characteristics (on-demand self-service, broad network access, resource pooling, rapid elasticity, measured service), three service models (cloud software as a service (SaaS), cloud platform as a service (PaaS), cloud infrastructure as a service (IaaS)) and four deployment models (private cloud, community cloud, public cloud, hybrid cloud).

- Gartner[16] considers cloud computing as a style of computing where massively scalable IT-related capabilities are provided "as a service" across the internet to multiple external customers.

- Forrester[17] sees cloud computing as a pool of abstracted, highly scalable, and managed infrastructure capable of hosting end-customer applications and billed by consumption.

- T-Systems, a german IT consulting company, defines cloud computing[18] [19] [20] as the renting of infrastructure and software, as well as bandwidths, under defined service conditions. These components should be able to be adjusted daily to the needs of the customer and offered with the upmost availability and security. Included in cloud computing are end-to-end service level agreements (SLAs) and use-dependent service invoices.

Other definitions and aspects of cloud computing can be found in the following bibliographic references[21] [22] [23] [24] [25]:

In general terms, cloud computing refers to offer solutions and applications to the end users without a need for installation and deployment in the own end user premises. A cloud computing service can be software as a service, which delivers the entire application. In the infrastructure as a service model[26], only the servers and operating systems are provided, and customers deploy their own applications on the hardware.

---

[15]See [36] National Institute of Standards and Technology: NIST Definition of Cloud Computing, <http://csrc.nist.gov/publications/nistpubs/800-145/SP800-145.pdf>, pp. 2-3

[16]See [29] Gartner research: Gartner says cloud computing will be as influential as E-business, <http://www.gartner.com/it/page.jsp?id=707508>

[17]See [27] Forrester Research: Cloud computing definition, <http://www.forrester.com/rb/research>

[18]See [16] T-Systems Enterprise Services, White Paper. Cloud Computing I, 2011

[19]See [17] T-Systems Enterprise Services, White Paper. Cloud Computing II, 2011

[20]See [18] T-Systems Enterprise Services, White Paper. Dynamic Services, 2011

[21]See [19] Van Zütphen, Thomas: Avancen aus der Wolke, 2011

[22]See [15] Terplan, Kornel; Voigt, Christian: Cloud Computing, 2011

[23]See [21] Velte, Anthony, et al: Cloud computing: A practical approach, 2010

[24]See [1] Baun, Christian; Kunze, Marcel: Cloud computing: Web-basierte dynamische IT-Services, 2010

[25]See [20] Van Zütphen, Thomas: Der CIO als Cloud-Broker, 2011

[26]See [39] PC magazine encyclopedia: Definition of cloud computing, 2012

Section 2.2.3 will explain in detail the existing cloud computing service models.

The cloud computing model is characterized by the benefits offered to the companies in terms of productivity, cost and flexibility. Cloud computing is seen as a trend with high potential to dominate the IT market due to the many advantages offered compared to current IT technologies. Nowadays, companies are forced to increase productivity, improve the cost structure and react faster to the changing market. By using cloud computing, companies benefit of the flexibility, scalability, price efficiency and mobility that can be reached with this service model.

Gartner research[27] estimates the cloud services revenue reached 68.3 US billion in 2010. Looking at the future, Gartner estimates the industry will strongly growth and reach a revenue of about 148.8 million by 2014.

2.2.2 Computer topology evolution

Over the last years, the computer topology moved from a monolithic and centralized environment based on mainframes to a distributed environments based on the client-server model. Recently, mesh environments are gaining importance. The mesh connectivity allows each system to communicate directly to others increasing the redundancy within the system. As a result, the data processing and storage may be shared between them in a dynamic manner. Figure 2.1[28] shows the computer topology evolution stages.

2.2.2.1 Mainframe

Mainframe computers[29] were introduced in the 1960s and consisted of centralized servers, which were deployed at customer's premises. This technology consisted of high available and performance computer systems that were very expensive and complex. Mainframes used normally the star network topology. This topology consists of computers connected directly to a mainframe.

Mainframes[30] were initially designed for big companies requiring the processing of high amount of information and data. Mainframes were scalable systems and connected to high-speed disk subsystems.

---

[27]See [28] Gartner research: Gartner Says Worldwide Cloud Services Market to Surpass $68 Billion in 2010, <http://www.gartner.com/it/page.jsp?id=1389313>

[28]See [14] Rhoton, John: Cloud Computing Explained, 2010, p. 31

[29]See [52] Wikipedia: Grossrechner, <http://de.wikipedia.org/wiki/Grossrechner, 2012>

[30]See [47] Webopedia, IT Business Edge: What is mainframe?, <http://www.webopedia.com/TERM/M/mainframe.html>

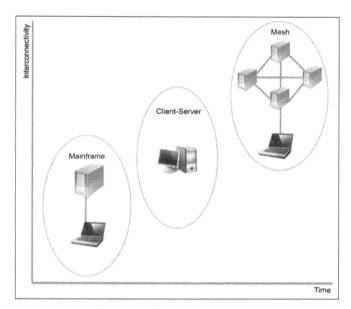

Figure 2.1: Connectivity evolution

2.2.2.2 Client-Server

The client-server model[31] introduced the possibility for a service requesters (also called client) to send tasks or workloads into a network for the further processing by service receivers (also called server). The servers receiving the requests process the information themselves or send it further to other computers connected to the network.

The servers in the client-server architecture[32] have high capacity and high performance for computing processing. This architecture provides a higher availability than the mainframe model as the clients are not only connected to one single server and in case of failover of one server, any other server connected to the network can process the information. The client-server model started to be used in the 1980s as applications were migrated from mainframes to networks of desktop computers.

2.2.2.3 Mesh topology

Finally, with the popularization of internet in the 1990s, the technology has seen an increased trend into the mesh connectivity. The mesh connectivity[33] allows that each

---

[31]See [48] Wikipedia: Client-server model,
<http://en.wikipedia.org/wiki/Client-server_model>
[32]See [38] PC magazine encyclopedia: Definition of client/server,
<http://www.pcmag.com/encyclopedia>
[33]See [14] Rhoton, John: Cloud Computing Explained, 2010, pp. 30-31

computer on the network can communicate to each other. Data processing, storage or any other computer process required can be dynamically shared and executed between systems. This model is highly scalable as the processes can be executed by distributed servers. Cloud computing bases on the mesh connectivity model.

Figure 2.2[34] summarizes the computer topology evolution and presents the main characteristics.

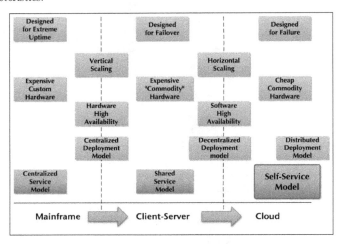

Figure 2.2: IT topology evolution

[34]See: [24] Bias, Randy: Debunking the "No Such Thing as A Private Cloud" Myth, <http://www.cloudscaling.com/blog/cloud-computing/debunking-the-no-such-thing-as-a-private-cloud-myth/>

2.2.3 Cloud computing service models

With the introduction of cloud computing, companies perceive the deployment of infrastructure and software applications in a different way. There is not longer a need to invest high amount of money buying expensive and redundant systems or purchasing a high number of software licenses.

Several services models are identified in cloud computing covering from infrastructure and database virtualization to user applications. As of today, three cloud computing service models are identified in the literature as the most relevant:

- Infrastructure as a service
- Platform as a service
- Software as a service

The most know payment model is the pay-as-you-go-model (PAYG)[35].

Figure 2.3[36] shows some applications for each cloud computing service model, which will be described in more detail in the following sections 2.2.3.1, 2.2.3.2 and 2.2.3.3.

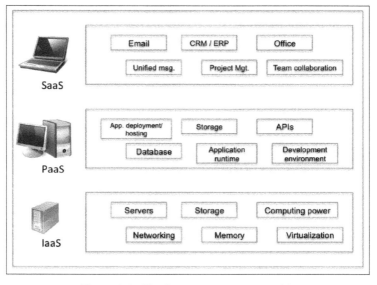

Figure 2.3: Cloud computing service models

[35]See [36] National Institute of Standards and Technology: NIST Definition of Cloud Computing, <http://csrc.nist.gov/publications/nistpubs/800-145/SP800-145.pdf>, 2011, pp. 2-3

[36]See [14] Rhoton, J.: Cloud Computing Explained, 2010, p. 22

2.2.3.1 Infrastructure as a Service

Infrastructure as a Service (IaaS)[37] operates at the lowest service level and refers to features including infrastructure like server, network, storage, memory and other computer related resources. Companies do not need to invest high amount of money purchasing, maintaining and operating an IT infrastructure as the complete infrastructure is operated and maintained by the cloud computing supplier. Additionally, companies can deploy any operating system and execute any application required. Cloud computing suppliers use the economies of scale by reducing the complexity of deploying a customer-specific infrastructure. Instead of this, a pool of servers and other infrastructure resources are setup and are made available to the companies. The term infrastructure as a service is also known as virtualization.
Figure 2.4[38] presents some different types of IaaS services.

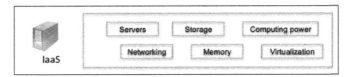

Figure 2.4: Infrastructure as a service stack

2.2.3.2 Platform as a Service

Platform as a Service model (PaaS)[39] operates at a higher level than infrastructure as a service. The platform as a service model provides the resources needed to develop, build, deploy, execute and maintain applications from the internet without the need to install the software in the own servers.
PaaS services include application design, development, testing, deployment and hosting. Figure 2.5[40] describes some further possible services applicable to PaaS.

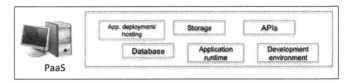

Figure 2.5: Platform as a service stack

---

[37]See [14] Rhoton, John: Cloud Computing Explained, 2010
[38]See [14] Rhoton, John: Cloud Computing Explained, 2010, pp. 13-14
[39]See [21] Velte , Anthony, et al: Cloud computing: a practical approach, 2010, p. 13
[40]See [14] Rhoton, John: Cloud Computing Explained, 2010, pp. 13-14

By adopting the PaaS service model[41], companies do not need to manage or control the underlying cloud infrastructure including network, servers, operating systems or storage, but they can still control the deployed applications and modify the configuration settings for the application-hosting environment.

2.2.3.3 Software as a Service

Software as a Service (SaaS)[42] is the most known and widest cloud computing service model used currently for the companies and people around the world. This model offers to customers business functionalities using the internet as enabler. Companies can use any software without installation at the own premises, without paying excessive and unnecessary license costs and without worrying about update installation and maintenance. The application can be accessed via internet using normally a web browser and independently of operating system or device used.

Figure 2.6[43] presents some applications covered by the SaaS model.

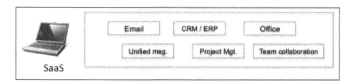

Figure 2.6: Software as a service stack

2.2.4 Advantages and limitations of cloud computing

2.2.4.1 Advantages of cloud computing

Adoption of cloud computing services brings many advantages for the companies[44]. The most important advantages of using cloud computing are described below:

- Possibility for the company to concentrate on core business
- There is not need for the company to invest resources in getting IT knowledge as the supplier brings its own expertise and specialized personal
- State-of-the-art solutions including infrastructure and software applications are always available as well as automatic updates
- Anywhere and anytime access independent of the device, computer or terminal used

---

[41]See [36] National Institute of Standards and Technology: NIST Definition of Cloud Computing, 2011, pp. 2-3

[42]See [21] Velte , Anthony, et al: Cloud computing: A practical approach, 2010, pp. 13-14

[43]See [14] Rhoton, John: Cloud Computing Explained, 2010, pp. 13-14

[44]See [10] Metzger, Christian, et all: Cloud computing, Chancen und Risiken aus technischer und unternehmerischer Sicht, 2011, p. 38f

- Reduction in the time to market due to factors such as the access to the latest technology
- High number of possible suppliers offers possibilities to reduce costs
- Economical advantages as there is no need for initial investment cost, reduction of operational cost and maintenance cost
- Cost efficiency is reached because the users of cloud computing only pay for the real service usage
- Multi-Tenancy plays an important economical aspect in terms of economies of scale. Adopting cloud computing services, users can share the same computing resources and there is not need to deploy a dedicated system for a unique user
- System scalability is one of the most important advantages of using cloud computing services. In case extra licenses or more servers are required, solution can be easily adapted to company's needs
- High system availability as agreed in service level agreements (SLAs) due to supplier's high performance systems
- Higher innovation potential by the use of state-of-the-art infrastructure, platforms and software. Companies benefit from the automatic updates performed directly from the suppliers
- Professional support by cloud computing supplier compared to small company.

2.2.4.2 Limitations of cloud computing

Following limitations[45] should be considered when adopting cloud computing services:

- Data security is considered the most important limitation and barrier factor for companies adopting cloud computing services. There are many constraints related to the security of information
- Correct functionality of infrastructure and software applications are highly dependent to internet access' availability and speed
- Companies implementing cloud computing services do not have the possibility to build up their own IT competence
- Adoption of cloud computing services adds high dependencies to supplier.

2.3 Fundamentals of success factors

2.3.1 Definition and characteristics

Success factors analysis[46] provides a set of variables with information where companies need to focus their resources and capabilities in order to succeed and gain

---

[45]See [10] Metzger, Christian, et all: Cloud computing, Chancen und Risiken aus technischer und unternehmerischer Sicht, 2011, p. 38f

[46]See [4] Grant, Robert: Contemporary strategy analysis, 2002, p. 100

competitive advantage in the market. The term success factor was defined initially by Chuck Hofer and Dan Schendel. They defined success factors[47] as "those variables that management can influence through its decisions and that can affect significantly the overall competitive positions of the firms in an industry. Within any particular industry they are derived from the interaction of two sets of variables, namely, the economic and technological characteristics of the industry and the competitive weapons on which the various firms in the industry have built their strategies".

Having knowledge of those success factors is not a guarantee for superior profitability but a good starting point to understand the industry environment and plan an effective business strategy[48], which will be used to allocate correctly the resources and capabilities in order to reach industry success.

Different studies[49] have been performed in order to provide empirical evidence of which business strategies lead to success and what are the key success factors. One of the most known studies is the profit impact of marketing strategy (PIMS) research program. The empirical investigation identified several strategic aspects that influence profitability. Among the most important strategic factors studied were market share, product quality, order of market entry and capital intensity. One of the most important results states the strategic factors are highly correlated with the profitability.

2.3.2 Methods to identify success factors

Based on Robert Grant's approach, two important aspects need to be considered for a company to succeed: The first aspect refers to knowing the customers and delivering them products they are willing to buy (see section 2.3.2.1). The second aspect consists of having a very good knowledge of the competition and its complex environment (see section 2.3.2.2). Figure 2.7[50] shows a basic framework introduced by Robert Grant which is used to identify key success factors.

2.3.2.1 Analysis of demand

The process of analysis of demand consists mainly in identifying who are the customers, what are their needs and what are the decision criteria they use to choose a particular product and company[51]. Once the factors have been identified, further analysis needs to be performed. For example, if customer's choice of software applications is based primarily in the data security and this is connected to the location

---

[47]See [5] Hofer, Chuck; Schendel, Dan: Strategy formulation: Analytical concepts, 1977, p. 77
[48]See [4]Grant, Robert, Contemporary strategy analysis, 2002, p. 100
[49]See [2] Buzzel, Robert: The PIMS program of strategy research. A retrospective appraisal, 2004
[50]See [4] p. 97
[51]See [4] p. 97

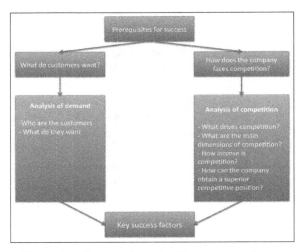

Figure 2.7: Framework to identify key success factors

of the servers, options related to server location offshore or in-customer-premises should be included into the offer by a cloud computing supplier.

Finally, Robert Grant refers in his book about the importance for a company to consider a customer not as a source of bargaining power but as a source of profit and as the main goal for the company's existence.

2.3.2.2 Analysis of competition

The second process consists on analyzing the current competition's situation in the industry[52]: how intense is the competition and what are its key dimensions. In the software market, consumers choose mainly the suppliers on the basis of market leadership and interoperability to existing systems. To reach this position, companies need to invest sufficiently enough resources in marketing advertising and product development.

2.4 Fundamentals of small- and medium-sized businesses

2.4.1 Definition and characteristics

Small- and medium-sized businesses play a very important social and economical role in many countries around the world[53]. As an example, 99% of the companies in the european union are represented by small- and medium-sized businesses. They provide around 90 million jobs and contribute to entrepreneurship and innovation.

---

[52]See [4] Grant, Robert, Contemporary strategy analysis, 2002, p. 97
[53]See [3] European Union: Commission recommendation concerning the definition of micro, small and medium-sized enterprises, 2003

The categorization of small- and medium-sized businesses is made based on the employees headcount and the revenues. The employees headcount is an initial criterion for determining in which category an small- and medium-sized business is located. It covers full-time, part-time and seasonal employes. The revenues is the second aspect to consider and it is determined by calculating the income that a company received during a year from its sales and services.

In general terms, small- and medium-sized businesses characterize for employing fewer than 250 persons and for having revenues not exceeding 50 million euro.

Typically, small-and medium-sized businesses are export-oriented, focus on innovative and high value manufactured products and have a worldwide domination of a niche market. They are typically privately owned and based in small rural communities. Many of the successful small-and medium-sized companies characterize for a long-term oriented approach with the adoption of modern management practices, like focusing on employee satisfaction, implementation of lean manufacturing practices and total quality management.

2.4.2   Definition of small- and medium-sized businesses

2.4.2.1   Small-sized businesses

Small-sized businesses are defined as companies employing fewer than 50 persons and with revenues not exceeding 10 million euro[54].

2.4.2.2   Medium-sized businesses

Medium-sized businesses consist of companies which employ fewer than 250 persons and which have revenues not exceeding 50 million euro[55].

---

[54]See [3] European Union: Commission recommendation concerning the definition of micro, small and medium-sized enterprises, 2003
[55]See [3]

CHAPTER 3

State-of-the-art research

This section presents some studies available in the literature, which focus on the adoption of cloud computing services at different companies including specially small- and medium-sized businesses.

3.1 Cloud computing in the insurance industry

A first investigation analyzed in scope of this book was the study performed by Fraunhofer - Institute for work management and organization[1] which investigated the role of cloud computing in the insurance market. This study was part of the research program THESEUS sponsored by the german economical and technological ministry.

The overall investigation consisted of two surveys. The first study was directed to the insurance companies and the second one to IT suppliers in the insurance market. In total, 15 insurance companies and 27 IT suppliers participated in the research. The small- and medium-sized companies in the insurance sector were represented by 4 insurance companies and 17 IT suppliers. The main goal of this research was to identify the potential adoption of cloud computing for this particular sector and the benefits and challenges of cloud computing services in the insurance market.

In general, the awareness level for topics related to cloud computing services is very high in insurance companies and their IT suppliers. From the supplier's side, a high interest for including cloud computing services in their portfolio was identified and one fifth of the suppliers are already offering cloud computing services. From user's point of view, the interest to adopt cloud computing services is very low: few insurance companies are currently using cloud computing services or even planning its use. In order to support the spreading of cloud computing technologies, a high effort directed to the companies, in form of guidance and consultancy, is required. Companies in the insurance market need to understand better the benefits and risks of adopting cloud computing services.

In regards to the key success factors, the topic security has a high relevance. Insurance companies as well as IT suppliers have many concerns to topics related to security. For that reason, it is important to focus on providing secure cloud computing technologies based on the state-of-the-art technologies in terms of security.

---

[1]See [23] Weidmann, Monika; Renner, Thomas; Rex, Sascha: Cloud computing in der Versicherungsbranche, 2010

Other important factors such as transparency from supplier's side and good communication, as well compliance to security standards and independently performed security audits play an important role. Another important aspect consists in making sure that a smooth integration and compatibility of the new cloud computing services into the existing systems is possible.

3.2 Cloud computing in the logistics sector

A second study in the area of cloud computing was performed by Fraunhofer-Institute for software and system techniques titled cloud computing for small- and medium-sized businesses in the logistics sector[2]. The focus of this investigation was to identify barriers for the adoption of cloud computing services and provide recommendations to cloud computing suppliers in order to overcome them.

In general, 60% of the decision makers in the logistics sector have plans to adopt cloud computing services and have a basic understanding of this new technology. The study refers as well to the key role of the cost saving factor. Logistic companies agreed in considering the cost transparency offered by adopting cloud services as an important factor as well the wide possibilities to track the costs and look continuously for improvements.

In regards to the relevant factors, companies consider there is a deficit in the information provided about cloud computing benefits, which can be solved with information campaigns which include best practice- and real use cases of cloud computing services working currently in different companies. The companies in the logistics sector consider: "the cloud computing technology might be there but there is not measurable and concrete facts based on the deployments available"[3]. A further important factor to consider relates to the interoperability to existing systems as well as the possibility to customize the solutions and integrate them with third-party solutions. Last but not least, the data security and the trust to the cloud computing supplier are considered by the logistic companies as important.

---

[2]See [9] Holtkamp, Berndhard: Cloud Computing für den Mittelstand am Beispiel der Logistikbranche, 2010
[3]See [9] p. 19

CHAPTER 4

Empirical survey

4.1 Objective

The empirical investigation done in scope of this book was performed in cooperation with the cloud computing business unit of Deutsche Telekom and had the main goal to identify the most relevant cloud computing solutions, which are planned to be adopted by small- and medium-sized businesses. The investigation helped as well to identify the level of acceptance and current usage of cloud computing services in small- and medium-sized businesses.

Another aspect investigated consists in identifying the most relevant aspects for the adoption of solutions based on the cloud computing model. Those aspects were used to identify the key success factors needed for the adoption of cloud computing services. Companies planning to adopt cloud computing based services were in focus. The empirical investigation includes 15 factors, which are important for a successful adoption of cloud computing services. These factors are organized in six different groups: security-, cost-, technology-, support- and supplier-related factors.

The empirical research investigates different aspects of cloud computing with the main focus on following questions:

- Is your company interested in using cloud computing services?
- Does your company already use cloud computing services?
- What cloud computing service model is currently being used at your company? What service model is planned to be used?
- What is the most relevant software as a service application your company is planning to use?
- What kind of service provider is your company using for the applications currently working?
- What are the most important aspects to consider when your company would plan to adopt a cloud computing service?

By identifying the most significant cloud computing applications and those key success factors relevant for the adoption of cloud computing services, it shall be feasible for a cloud computing supplier to effectively offer the specific applications fulfilling the necessary requirements.

4.2 Method

The empirical investigation consists of an online survey with a participation of 613
employees working as IT decision makers in different industry sectors. The employees represent companies with a number of employees ranging from 1 to 249. Based
on the definition for small-and medium-sized businesses as described in section 2.4.2,
companies were segmented as follows: 432 companies fulfilled the requirements of
small-sized businesses, 148 companies were identified as medium-sized companies.
33 of the companies interviewed could not be categorized in the small- and medium-
sized businesses as they did not fulfill the requisites in terms of revenues. In total,
580 companies were identified as small- and medium-sized businesses and the empirical investigation done in scope of this book based on this figure.
The industries included in the investigation were:

- IT and technology
- Professional services
- Consultancy
- Retail
- Financial services
- Building industry
- Law, audit
- Media, publishing
- Healthcare
- Electronics
- Automotive
- Logistics
- Mechanical engineering
- Telecommunications

The participants were asked about the current applications being used at their
companies, about the acceptance of cloud services, the plans to include cloud services
in the company, the requirements and barriers to be considered for the adoption of
cloud computing services. The survey had a duration of around 15 minutes and was
performed in the dates from 13th to 23rd of December 2011. The most relevant
questions for this book are included in the appendix A in the page 63.

4.3 Sample

This section provides the most important information about the small- and medium-sized companies participating in the empirical research. Aspects like the industry distribution, the number of employees and the revenues are described in the following sections.

4.3.1 Industry distribution

Figures 4.1 and 4.2 show the industry distribution of the small- and medium-sized companies, which have participated in the survey.

For the small-sized companies segment, companies representing technology, professional services, consultancy and retail branches cover 49% of the companies interviewed. The total number of small-sized businesses is 432.

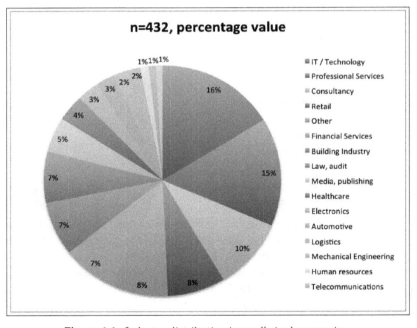

Figure 4.1: Industry distribution in small-sized companies

The medium-sized companies are dominated by companies working in the area of technology, mechanical engineering, professional services, retail, building industry and electronics (59%). 148 medium-sized companies have participated in this survey.

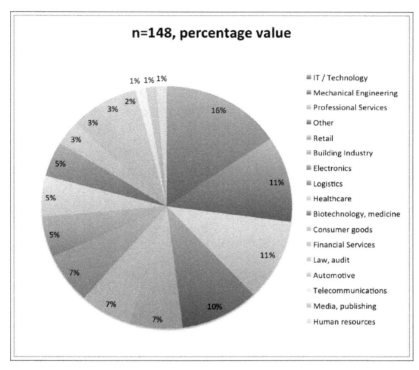

Figure 4.2: Industry distribution in medium-sized companies

4.3.2 Employees distribution

From the small-sized businesses, companies with fewer than 5 employees represented 58% of the interviewed companies as shown in the figure 4.3.

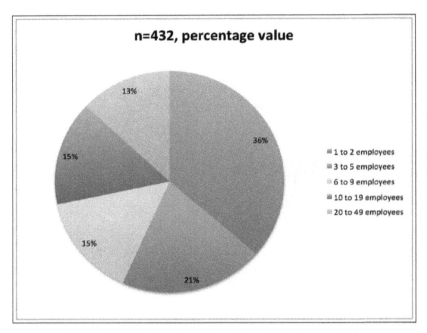

Figure 4.3: Number of employees in small-sized companies

In figure 4.4 it can be identified, the medium-sized business group is dominated by companies with a number of employees ranging from 50 to 250 and representing 90% of the interviewed companies.

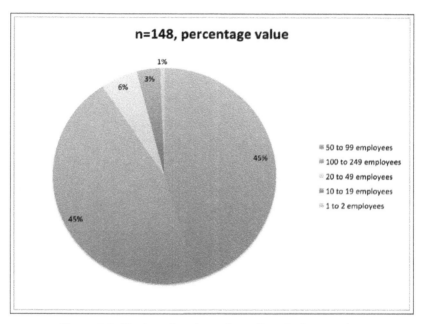

Figure 4.4: Number of employees in medium-sized companies

4.3.3 Revenues distribution

Revenues for small-sized companies have in a range from less than 500 thousand euro to 10 million euro. The figure 4.5 shows that a high percent of the small-sized companies (58%) has revenues below 500 thousand euro.

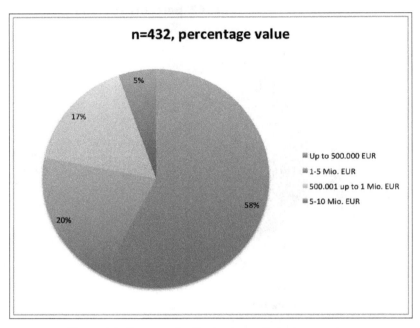

Figure 4.5: Revenue distribution in small-sized companies

In the case of medium-sized businesses, 71% of the companies has revenues ranging between 5 and 50 million euro. Figure 4.6 shows the whole distribution of medium-size businesses based on the revenues.

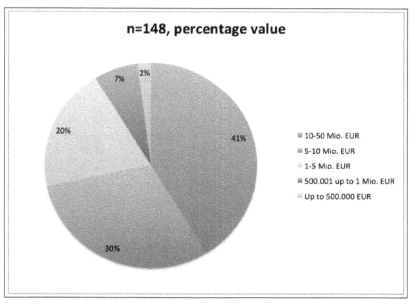

Figure 4.6: Revenue distribution in medium-sized companies

CHAPTER 5

Analysis of cloud computing applications for small- and medium-sized businesses

5.1 Acceptance and usage of cloud computing

5.1.1 Acceptance of cloud computing

The empirical investigation based on the online survey as presented in section 4.2 shows similar results of cloud computing acceptance for small- and medium-sized businesses. Basically, companies have a neutral position in terms of implementing cloud computing services in a short-term. 36% of the small-sized businesses neither reject the use of cloud computing services nor plan the use yet. Similar results are available for medium-sized business with 34% located in this segment.

Unexpectedly, there is a high tendency in small- and medium-sized businesses for not considering the use of cloud computing services. 36% of small and 27% of medium-sized businesses consider the use of cloud computing services as an irrelevant topic for the companies.

Results also exhibit a lack of knowledge for cloud computing topics as 11% of the small-sized businesses hear about the new technology for the first time. Companies belonging to the medium-sized businesses group have more knowledge about cloud computing technologies and the term cloud computing is new for only 5% of them. On the other hand, 10% of the small-sized businesses plan to use cloud services in the near future compared to 23% of the medium-sized group. It can also be identified that 7% of the small-sized businesses and 11% of the medium-sized businesses are using cloud services already. Figure 5.1 and figure 5.2 present the complete results in term of acceptance of cloud services.

In general, there is a higher acceptance for cloud computing services in medium-sized businesses and a significant lack of knowledge in small-sized businesses. Based on this information, a need to educate and increase the awareness in small-sized business in terms of cloud computing was identified.

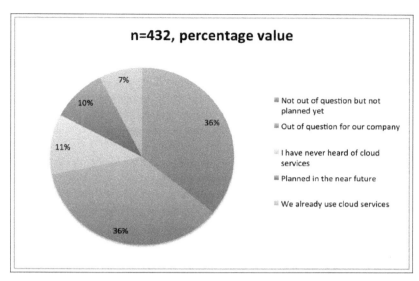

Figure 5.1: Acceptance of cloud computing services in small-sized businesses

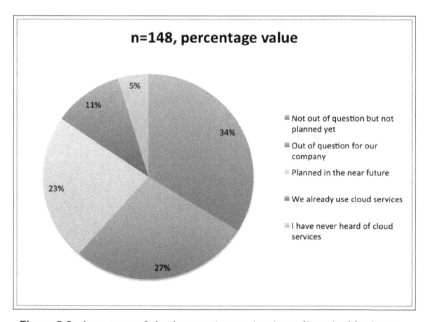

Figure 5.2: Acceptance of cloud computing services in medium-sized businesses

5.1.2 Usage of cloud services models

Based on the results of cloud computing acceptance previously presented, the usage of each cloud computing service model was also questioned. The focus now is to identify the current use and the plans for using any of the cloud computing service models. Only the companies showing either an interest in cloud computing service or already using them have been asked. Companies rejecting the usage of cloud computing services were out of scope. In total, 230 out of 432 small-sized companies have shown interest in cloud computing services and 100 out of 148 of the medium-sized companies.

From the results it can be identified small- and medium-sized businesses have a special interest in the software as a service model. 42% of the small-sized businesses are planning to use the software as a service model and 8% already used it. In the medium-sized business group, 53% are planning to use a software as a service application and 16% are already using one.

Infrastructure as a service represents the second most relevant cloud computing service model: 39% of small-sized businesses and 47% of the medium-sized businesses are considering to use infrastructure as a service as an alternative to the traditional model.

Finally, the platform as a service model appears to be the least relevant as 63% of the small-sized companies and 51% of the medium-sized companies are not planning to use a solution based on this model. The results surprisedly show a current use of platform as a service in medium-sized businesses. 13% of the medium-sized businesses are currently using the platform as a service model contrarily to small-sized businesses using the model only 4% of the companies. Results are shown in the figures 5.3 and 5.4.

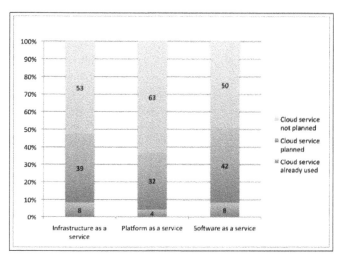

Figure 5.3: Usage in small-sized businesses (n=230, percentage value)

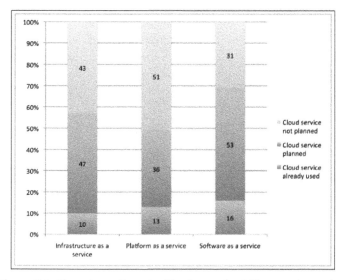

Figure 5.4: Usage in medium-sized businesses (n=100, percentage value)

Summarizing the survey's results in terms of acceptance and usage, there is a general interest in the small-and medium-sized companies to adopt cloud computing services and cloud computing technologies are well accepted in the industry, however a lack of information for topics related to cloud computing was identified. It is worth to mention, when companies were asked about the cloud computing definition, employees of small- and medium-sized companies frequently connected the term cloud computing to the new cloud services, which are being promoted recently by Apple and Deutsche Telekom such as iCloud and TelekomCloud.

There is still a big gap to be filled with consultancy and intensive information sessions as part of a business development strategy to accelerate the decision process at the companies. The consultancy should concentrate on informing the companies about the immense opportunities and advantages by adopting cloud computing services, as well as the limitations and constraints and the different alternatives to overcome them.

Finally, the empirical investigation shows software as a service solution is the cloud computing service with the highest acceptance among the small- and medium-sized companies. The next sections will present the results in terms of cloud computing services with a main focus on software as a service applications as this cloud computing model is gaining high importance within companies.

In addition, marketplaces are becoming more known and a new option for the companies. The term marketplace[1] is used in cloud computing terminology to describe a unique place where companies can find a collection of cloud computing applications. Currently, there is a small selection of marketplaces available which include the marketplace from Salesforce[2] and the Google Marketplace[3].

Specifically for the german market there is an initiative called "initiative cloud services made in Germany "[4] with the purpose of centralizing the cloud computing applications .

5.2 Cloud computing solutions

5.2.1 Infrastructure as a service solution

Infrastructure as a service is an interesting option for small- and medium-sized companies willing to use virtual servers for data processing and storage instead of operating their own servers.

---

[1]See [30] Göldie, Andreas: Google macht Ernst mit Cloud Computing, <http://netzwertig.com/2010/03/11/app-marketplace-google-macht-ernst-mit-enterprise-cloud-computing>

[2]See [42] Salesforce: The cloud computing marketplace from Salesforce, <http://appexchange.salesforce.com/home>

[3]See [32] Google: Google Apps Marketplace, <http://www.google.com/enterprise/marketplace>

[4]See [33] Grohmann, Werner: Initiative Cloud Services Made in Germany, <http://www.cloud-services-made-in-germany.de>

The adoption of the infrastructure as a service model brings many benefits to the companies: there is no need for purchasing any server infrastructure as the servers are located remotely in the supplier's premises. Companies benefit from the scalability and system dimensioning of the systems and the lower operational, administrative and maintenance cost compared to the traditional method.

There are however some limitations to consider when adopting infrastructure as a service solution like the dependance on the internet availability and speed and the potential integration costs to the infrastructure currently available.

The next sections present the results of the empirical investigation covering the infrastructure as a service model. The number of companies using infrastructure as a service solutions is low based on the survey: 19 small-sized businesses and 10 medium-sized businesses.

5.2.1.1   Storage

Storage refers to a supplier renting storage capacity to end users[5]. The storage service has gained importance due to the increased complexity of backup, replication and disaster recovery at the companies, especially in small- and medium-sized companies.

The empirical investigation shows similar results for the current usage of storage in small- and medium-sized businesses. Figure 5.5 and 5.6 show that the infrastructure as a service model is dominated by the storage service as 89% of the small- and 80% of the medium-sized businesses are using the service.

5.2.1.2   Processing / Computing power

The term processing or computing power refers to the possibility to rent servers for performing computational processes.

The figures 5.5 and 5.6 show the usage of processing power services in medium-sized companies of 20% compared to 5% at small-sized companies.

In general terms, the infrastructure as a service model plays an insignificant role as cloud computing model. In case an adoption is planned, storage as a service needs to be considered as interesting solution for small- and medium-sized businesses.

---

[5]See [21] Velte , Anthony, et al: Cloud computing: A practical approach, 2010, p. 136

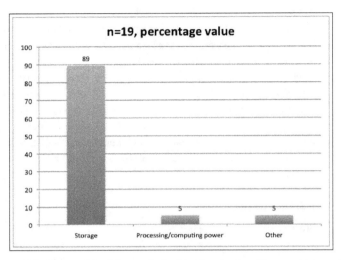

Figure 5.5: Usage of IaaS in small-sized businesses (n=19, percentage value)

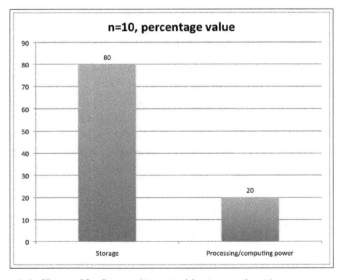

Figure 5.6: Usage of IaaS in medium-sized businesses (n=10, percentage value)

5.2.2   Platform as a Service solution

Platform as a service has a relevance for companies building their own applications and hosting them without purchasing a development platform or a hosting server as they are located at the cloud supplier's side. Using platform as a service solutions, companies benefit from renting the state-of-the-art development platform available, increasing also the time to market and avoiding high initial cost. Some limitations like the new dependencies to the cloud supplier or some initial effort required in the customization need to be considered.

Following sections summarize the results of the empirical investigation.

5.2.2.1   Application deployment and hosting

The application deployment and hosting service enables users to deploy and run applications remotely using the cloud suppliers infrastructure. Despite the low number of companies currently using platform as a service solutions (10 small-sized businesses and 13 medium-sized businesses, the result shows a tendency at small- and medium-sized businesses of using application deployment and hosting service as shown in the figures 5.7 (50% of the small-sized companies) and figure 5.8 (69% of the medium-sized companies). Specifically, the service Microsoft Azure was mentioned several times when asked about the platform as a service model.

5.2.2.2   Storage

The storage service refers to the possibility to store and manage the own applications on the cloud supplier servers. Companies benefit of the backup and redundancy functionalities of the cloud computing supplier. The storage service is the second most used platform as a service model and has more relevance in small-sized businesses (40%) than in medium-sized businesses (8%).

5.2.2.3   Development environment

The development environment allows companies to develop, build and run applications. Normally the platform as a service include an operating system and developer tools. This solution has a low significance in small-sized businesses with a usage of 10%. At the other side, it has a higher relevance for medium-sized businesses as 23% of the interviewed companies are using this solution.

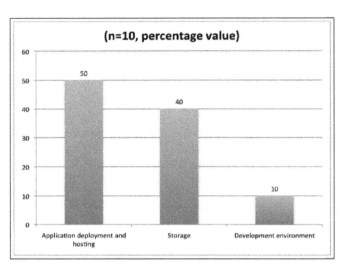

Figure 5.7: Usage of PaaS in small-sized businesses (n=10, percentage value)

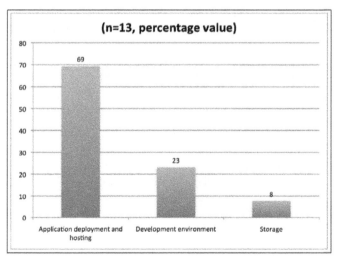

Figure 5.8: Usage of PaaS in medium-sized businesses (n=13, percentage value)

5.2.3 Software as a Service solution

The software as a service segment is the most known and prevalent cloud computing service used in the industry. Apart from the general cloud computing advantages, companies benefit from the cost transparency and cost reduction, the easy scalability, high availability and the possibility for device independent access of the software. Despite of this, the security of the company's information represents the key constraint for the adoption of software as a service applications.

The following sections show the results of the empirical investigation, which was presented in section 4.2. The results provide information about the type of software as a service application planned to be adopted in the companies. Figure 5.9 and 5.10 present the results of the survey. In total, 107 small-sized businesses and 67 medium-sized businesses use applications based on cloud computing model.

It is important to identify the current software application supplier as the switching cost play a key role for the adoption of a new system. As defined by Michael Porter[6], switching costs are fixed cost that buyers face when they change supplier. Such costs may arise because a buyer switching a vendor must, for example, alter product specifications, train employees to use the new system, or modify processes or information systems. Information about the current suppliers preference is briefly discussed and discussed in this section.

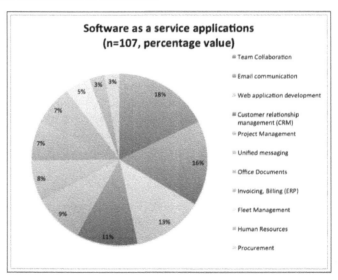

Figure 5.9: Most relevant SaaS applications in small-sized businesses

---

[6]See [13] Porter, Michael E.: The five competitive forces that shape strategy, 2008, p. 4

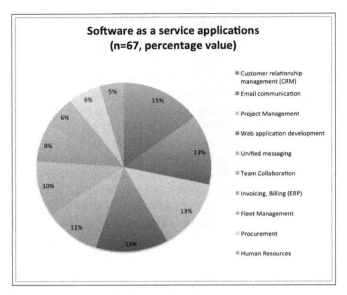

Figure 5.10: Most relevant SaaS applications in medium-sized businesses

5.2.3.1 Team collaboration

As described in section 2.1.2.4, team collaboration software refers to centralized document sharing platforms for easy access from team members.

Team collaboration applications represent the first position of preference for software as as service applications among small-sized companies. 18% of the small-sized businesses are planning to adopt team collaboration applications as a software as a service compared to 10% of the medium-sized businesses.

Regarding the top providers for team collaboration applications, Dropbox and Microsoft Sharepoint are used in many of the companies interviewed.

5.2.3.2 Email communication

Email communication refers to applications for use of email services (see section 2.1.2.1). Email communication as software as a service has an important relevancy in the small-and medium-sized companies and is positioned at the second place of preference for small- and medium-sized business with 16% and 13% respectively.

It was identified, the email communication software market is clearly dominated by Microsoft Outlook.

5.2.3.3   Web development

Web development software refers to applications for development of internet websites (see further definition in section 2.1.2.7).

Web development software has an increasing importance and there is a high level of acceptance of adopting the software as a service model. 13% of small-sized businesses and 13% of the medium-sized businesses plan to adopt the model in short-term.

The web development software market is shared between two companies, Adobe and Microsoft with the products Adobe Dreamweaver and Microsoft WebMatrix.

5.2.3.4   Customer relationship management

Customer relationship management tools are used to manage customer information and use it in order to improve the customer interaction (see section 2.1.2.5). Customer relationship management as software as a service has a very high relevance in medium-sized businesses and locates in the first place of relevance with 15% of the companies planning to shift to the cloud computing model. In terms of small-sized businesses, the software has a moderate 11% of relevance.

Currently, small-and medium-sized businesses are using traditional software from two main suppliers, Microsoft Dynamics and SAP CRM.

5.2.3.5   Project management

Project management software is used in companies for all activities related to coordination of projects (see section 2.1.2.3). The usage of project management software as cloud service is different for small- and medium-sized businesses. While the cloud computing service is relevant for medium-sized businesses with 13% of relevance and locating in the second place of preference, the service was selected by 9% of the small-sized companies.

With respect to the current usage, Microsoft Project dominates clearly the market and most of the companies are using the stand-alone software.

5.2.3.6   Unified messaging

Unified messaging software is used for improving the communication within the company and consists of a set of applications such as instant messaging, web conferencing and presence (refer to section 2.1.2.8).

The empirical investigation exhibits similar results for small- and medium-sized businesses and positions the software as a service model for unified messing in a medium significance level. Only 8% and 11% of the small- and medium-sized businesses are planning to adopt the cloud computing model.

Concerning the stand-alone solutions currently deployed in the companies, the market is shared among Skype and Microsoft Lync.

5.2.3.7 Office documents

The office document software segment applies to applications used for word processing, spreadsheet calculations, preparation of slides and database processing (refer to section 2.1.2.2).

Surprisingly, the relevance of office document software based on software as a service is not well accepted and companies are not planning to move the current application into the new technology. Only 7% of the small-sized businesses are considering the use of this new model. Medium-sized businesses are not planning the shift at all as none (0%) of the companies are planning to adopt the cloud model.

Regarding the market share of current office document software used, Microsoft Office dominates clearly the market.

5.2.3.8 Enterprise resource planning

Enterprise resource planning software is used to centralize and manage the aspects related to the value chain of a company (see section 2.1.2.9).

The adoption of this type of software as software as a service is not well accepted. Only 7% of the small-sized businesses and 8% of the small-sized business are planning to adopt the cloud model. Companies stated as main reason for the low usage data security concerns.

The market of stand-alone applications in small-and medium-sized businesses is dominated by Lexware and SAP.

5.2.3.9 Fleet management

As described in section 2.1.2.10, fleet management software is used for managing the aspects related to a fleet of vehicles.

Fleet management based on the software as a service model has a very low significance with only 5% and 6% of the small- and medium-sized businesses planning to use the cloud model, respectively.

The market of stand-alone software for fleet management in small-and medium-sized businesses in Germany is dominated mainly by german companies such as Lexware and WISO.

5.2.3.10 Human resource management

Human resource management software supports the activities related to management of employee information (refer to section 2.1.2.11).

This type of software has a low relevance and the plans for adopting the application as cloud model are very low. 3% of small- and 5% of medium-sized companies have plans to shift the existing applications into the new technology.

The current market share of stand-alone applications in small-and medium-sized businesses is divided between Lexware and SAP.

Summarizing, the most relevant applications most likely to be adopted by small-sized businesses based on the empirical investigation are:

- Software for team collaboration, email communication and web development play a key role and have the highest possibility to be adopted by small-sized companies at short-term
- The second group of relevance consists of software applications for customer relationship management, project management and unified messaging
- Finally, software applications in the area of office documentation, enterprise resource planning, fleet management, human resources and procurement have currently an insignificant role.

Concerning the adoption of cloud computing applications at medium-sized businesses based on the software as a service model, the empirical investigation shows the following results:

- Customer Relationship Management, email communication, project management and web development have the first place in relevance
- A second group of relevance consists of software applications for unified messaging, team collaboration and enterprise resource planning
- Software applications related to fleet management, procurement and human resources have the least level of significance.

Analysis of success factors for cloud computing for small- and medium-sized businesses

6.1 Security related factors

6.1.1 Overview

This section evaluates the importance of security-related factors in small- and medium-sized businesses as determinant for the adoption of cloud computing services. Security related factors consist of three factors such as data security, data storage in Germany and security audits. The research results are presented in the figures 6.1 and 6.2.The number of companies, which selected security related factors, consists of 216 small-sized businesses and 117 medium-sized businesses.

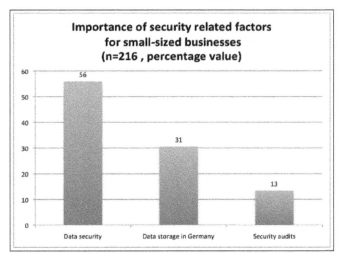

Figure 6.1: Security related factors for small-sized businesses

6.1.2 Data security

A high number of companies participating in the empirical investigation consider the data security as a very important factor. The results for small- and medium-sized

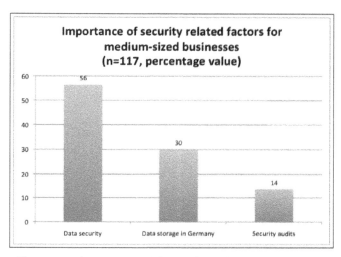

Figure 6.2: Security related factors for medium-sized businesses

business are identical. 56% of the companies placed data security as the first factor of importance concerning security.

The importance of data security is very well understood by cloud computing suppliers and is identified as one of the main constraints for the adoption of cloud computing solutions by companies. For this reason, cloud computing suppliers need to increase the transparency in terms of information regarding security aspects by including details in their offers such as the compliance to existing industry security standards (ISO 27001, EU model clauses, etc.). Additionally, the available policies, the different layers of security used, the proactive and continuos data monitoring in order to identify potential malicious access and the access restriction to production servers facilitate as well a high transparency.

6.1.3 Data storage in Germany

Companies interviewed consider the data location as an essential factor. Cloud computing suppliers shall offer guarantees about data storage in the local country, in this case, Germany, as the empirical research was directed uniquely to companies located in Germany. The adoption of cloud computing services in small- and medium-sized businesses relates not only to the data storage in Germany but also to provide transparent information about who has access to the information.

6.1.4 Security audits

Unexpectedly, the results of the empirical investigation show the lowest values for the factors related to security audits. Companies are not expecting regular controls from certified organization such as TÜV and see this aspect as the least important. This result has a relevancy for the cloud computing suppliers and can rely on the fact, that companies consider the credibility and transparency from cloud computing suppliers as an essential factor.

6.2 Cost related factors

6.2.1 Overview

Cost-related factors play an essential role as a factor for adopting cloud solutions and is considered as one of the most important benefits for using cloud computing services.

This section evaluates the importance of cost-related factors in small- and medium-sized businesses by analyzing following factors: low cost and cost transparency.

Figures 6.3 and 6.4 present the results for the cost-related factors for 191 small-sized businesses and 105 medium-sized businesses.

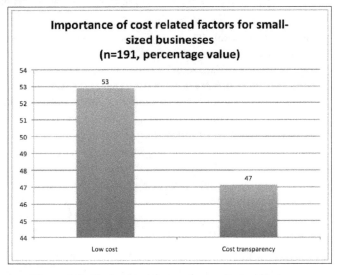

Figure 6.3: Cost related factors for small-sized businesses

6.2.2 Low cost

Cost savings translated to aspects such as low initial investment, low operational cost and low maintenance cost are key decision factors for small- and medium-sized businesses planning to adopt cloud computing services. Companies benefit from the economies of scale in term of technology solutions offered by cloud computing

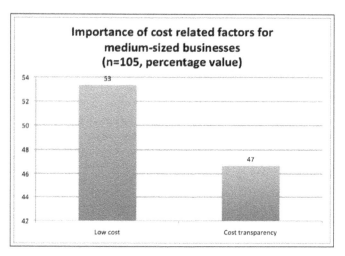

Figure 6.4: Cost related factors for medium-sized businesses

suppliers. The results of the survey show similar values for the group of companies interviewed: 53% relevance for small-sized businesses and 53% relevance for medium-sized businesses.

It is important to mention, companies planning to use cloud computing services are familiar with the benefits of cloud computing in terms of cost savings and they consider this factor as one of the key advantages of this technology.

6.2.3 Price transparency

Price or cost transparency has a remarkable position as a cost factor for the adoption of cloud computing services and are very high rated in the empirical investigation's results. Companies consider important to be able to track and understand the actual cost of the used solutions. Cloud services makes feasible to track the actual cost as the services base on the pay-as-you-go billing model.

6.3 Technology related factors

6.3.1 Overview

The questions related to technology related factors show slightly different results. In general, service stability and interoperability to existing systems are considered as the most relevant factors for small- and medium-sized businesses. Features related to customization have lower importance in small-sized businesses, fomented by factors like cost savings as a result of the economies of scale achieved with cloud computing. Those factors were identified and presented in the previous section as main focus for companies adopting cloud computing services and particularly in the early stages of implementation.

Results related to technology related factors are presented in figure 6.5 and figure 6.6 for 196 small-sized businesses and 101 medium-sized businesses, which considered technology related factors as important.

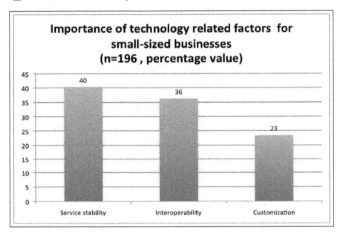

Figure 6.5: Technology related factors for small-sized businesses

6.3.2 Service stability

The service stability factor has a slightly higher relevance for small-sized businesses than for medium-sized businesses, however the factor is located in the first two places of importance in terms of technology for both groups: 40% of small-sized businesses considered the factor as relevant compared to 32% of medium-sized businesses. Smooth functionality must be guaranteed and a stable and reliable framework around the cloud services must be available. Factors like stability and speed of the internet connection are additional variables not present in stand-alone solutions. Cloud computing suppliers need to cooperate with internet providers in order to guarantee high availability and superior internet connection to the adopters of cloud computing services.

6.3.3 Interoperability

Interoperability to existing systems has a higher importance for medium-sized businesses. A reason may be related to the existence of a more established infrastructure in medium-sized business compared to small-sized businesses, which results also in more concerns regarding interoperability and migration costs: higher interoperability efforts lead to higher migration costs. These costs will have an impact on the

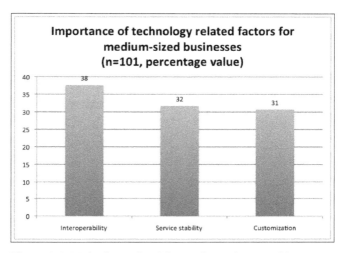

Figure 6.6: Technology related factors for medium-sized businesses

cloud computing adoption decision. Adoption of cloud computing services will success whether a smooth interoperability to existing systems is guaranteed. The factor interoperability was selected by 36% of small-sized businesses and 38% of medium-sized businesses as relevant.

6.3.4 Customization

The economies of scale and the effects in the possibilities of customization are well understood by small-sized companies. The customization factor plays an insignificant role for this group (23%).

In terms of medium-sized businesses, the relatively high relevance might be connected to a more advanced, complex and specialized infrastructure (31%).

6.4 Support related factors

6.4.1 Overview

The relevance of support related factors is similar for small-and medium-sized businesses based on the empirical investigation. A permanent support via phone and email preferably in german language is expected. As a result of the new technologies and the wide internet usage, cloud computing suppliers can guarantee this permanent support.

On-site support is considered by around one third of the small-and medium-sized businesses as important, followed by support in the setup and migration.

A summary of the factors is shown in the figures 6.7 and 6.8 for 137 small-sized businesses and 82 medium-sized businesses.

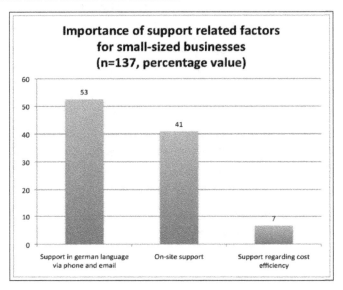

Figure 6.7: Support related factors for small-sized businesses

6.4.2 Support in german language via phone and email

A contact person for support in case of difficulties in the form of a hotline or email plays a key role for the adoption of cloud computing services. It is very important for the cloud computing suppliers to guarantee this support to the small-and medium sized businesses in questions facing the whole adoption process such as planning, setting-up, deployment and execution of the cloud computing services. The support shall be preferably in german language. The factor was selected by more than half of the companies: 53% of small-sized businesses and 51% of medium-sized businesses.

6.4.3 On-site support

On-site support has the second place of relevance and is mainly needed during the implementation phase when the cloud computing solutions must be integrated to the current company's infrastructure.

On-site support is connected to the presence of the company in the local country, in this case, the company having the headquarter or a subsidiary in Germany. 41% of the small-sized businesses and 40% of the medium-sized businesses considered the on-site support as important.

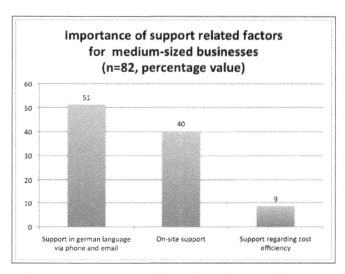

Figure 6.8: Support related factors for medium-sized businesses

6.4.4 Support regarding cost efficiency

The last position within the support related factors consists of support in early stages of the adoption process. Cost reduction needs to be verifiable and an offer around answering questions related to the verification of cost saving needs to be available. This verification can be supported with methods such as the total cost of ownership method.

6.5 Supplier related factors

6.5.1 Overview

None of the analyzed factors delivered such different results in terms of significance as the supplier related factors. However, the factors were equally distributed and each one represents approximately one forth of the overall results.
Figures 6.9 and 6.10 exhibit the empirical results for supplier related factors for 109 small-sized businesses and 69 medium-sized businesses.

6.5.2 Headquarter in Germany

Small-and medium-sized businesses agreed about the importance of the origin of the cloud computing supplier and the preference of selecting a supplier with headquarters in Germany. Not only a big german company is preferred but also a regional partner. The empirical investigation gives information about the very low preference of small-

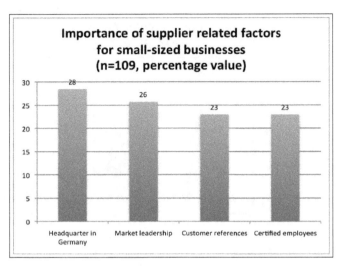

Figure 6.9: Supplier related factors for small-sized businesses

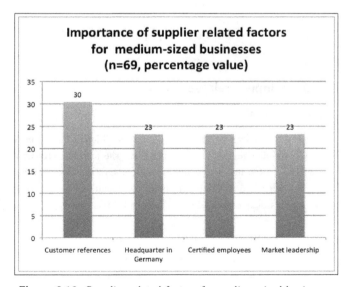

Figure 6.10: Supplier related factors for medium-sized businesses

and medium-sized companies for selecting foreign cloud suppliers specially from the USA, which is a result of the low reputation they have in terms of security in Germany. 28% of small-sized businesses and 23% of medium-sized businesses consider a cloud computing supplier with headquarter in Germany as important.

6.5.3 Customer references

The factor related to customer references has a more important role for medium-sized (30%) than for small-sized businesses (23%) occupying the first place of relevance. Medium-sized businesses expect from the cloud computing suppliers an already gained reputation and trust with respect to other companies and specially with the DAX companies. Customer references include a wide range of aspects as for example professionalism, customer service and exactitude to fulfill deadlines and budget estimations.

6.5.4 Certified employees

The aspect of cloud computing suppliers having employees holding original equipment certifications is not seen as a relevant factor neither for small-sized nor for medium-sized companies. This can be related to other factors, which have more importance such as trust to the cloud computing supplier.

6.5.5 Market leadership

Market leadership has a slightly more relevance for small-sized businesses than for medium-sized businesses. In general terms, the factor is not relevant at all as the empirical investigation reveals the importance of some other factors when the adoption of cloud computing services is planned.

Summarizing, the most relevant factors concerning the adoption of cloud computing services in small-and medium sized businesses based on the empirical investigation are:

- The aspect concerning data security occupies the first place of relevance and it is considered a critical factor influencing the decision to adopt the cloud computing service
- Companies understand the benefits of cloud computing in terms of cost transparency and the lower cost compared to stand-alone solutions. The cost saving related factors are well accepted by the companies
- Despite the high advances in terms of technology, companies have concerns regarding new dependencies which are added in the adoption of cloud computing technologies such as dependencies to the internet availability and internet speed

- The empirical results exhibit the importance of permanent support to accompany the small- and medium-sized companies during the whole adoption process including preferably support in german language
- There is a high tendency to prefer local suppliers with good references of previous cloud computing deliveries.

CHAPTER 7

Conclusions

Services based on the cloud computing model are gaining more and more importance and in a short-term, they are planned to change considerably the way, companies are managing currently their IT resources. Nowadays, companies are facing a increased and more complexed number of challenges and the need to overcome them in shorter time and with limited financial and personal resources are getting more relevant to success in the industry.

The adoption of cloud computing brings many possibilities to the current organization in terms of adapt the scalability, optimization of resource allocation, cost flexibility, use of state-of-the-art technologies and faster time-to-market.

The empirical investigation performed in the scope of this book and the available research analyzed exhibit similar results. The adoption of cloud computing technologies is well accepted and there is a high interest to adopt solutions based on cloud computing in small- and medium-sized businesses.

In terms of cloud computing solutions, the software as a service solution was identified as the cloud computing service with the most acceptance in the small- and medium-sized companies, followed by the infrastructure as a service model.

Regarding the preference for software as a service applications, it was identified by the survey, small- and medium-sized businesses have plans to adopt cloud computing applications in areas for improving the communication within the companies and the employees' mobility such as team collaboration and unified messaging solutions, as well as supporting the daily work such as project management and email communication solutions. Applications involving sensitive company's and customer's information such as enterprise resource planning, procurement and human resource applications have the least preference and the short-term adoption is not planned.

When focusing on key success factors, security related factors represents an important concern for companies planning to adopt cloud computing services. Small- and medium-sized companies expect from cloud computing suppliers transparency and credibility with the handling of information. Cost saving and cost transparency obtained with the adoption of cloud computing services have also high importance in small-and medium-sized companies. The benefits of economy of scale and possibility to concentrate on the core business are well accepted in the companies analyzed. Further factors identified in the scope of the empirical investigation are concerns related to the internet connection as a new enabler for cloud computing applications, the requirements in terms of support in the local language and the preference for local suppliers.

Additionally, the empirical investigation identified a general lack of information about topics concerning best practices for the adoption of cloud computing services including also the evaluation of adoption costs and risks. This gap in terms of information can be filled with professional consultancy and intensive information sessions as part of a business development strategy in order to accelerate the decision process in the companies. The importance of this aspect is already understood by some cloud computing suppliers, which affirmed, the sales effort is spent, most of the time, providing consultancy to the potential cloud computing adopters.

Online survey

A.1 Screening

A.1.1 Frage S1

Zu welcher der folgenden Branchen gehört das Unternehmen, in dem Sie tätig sind?
Bitte zutreffende Antwort anklicken.

1. Automobil
2. Konsumgüterhersteller
3. Finanzdienstleistungen
4. Rechts- und Steuerberatung, Wirtschaftsprüfung
5. Professionelle Dienstleistungen
6. IT / Technologie
7. Handel
8. Telekommunikation
9. Logistik und Verkehr
10. Gesundheitswesen
11. Bauwirtschaft
12. Biotechnologie, Chemie, Pharmazie und Medizin
13. Elektronik, Elektrotechnik, Technik
14. Maschinen- und Anlagenbau
15. Medien, Verlag, Druck
16. Personaldienstleistungen, Arbeitsvermittlung
17. Unternehmensberatung

A.1.2 Frage S2

In welchem Ausmaß sind Sie in Ihrem Unternehmen an Entscheidungen über die
EDV/IT beteiligt? Bitte zutreffende Antwort anklicken.

1. Ich bin der Hauptentscheider / einer der Hauptentscheider, wenn es um solche Technologien geht
2. Ich bin Mitentscheider, wenn es um solche Technologien geht
3. Ich nehme bei solchen Technologien keinen Einfluss auf die Entscheidung

A.1.3 Frage S9

Wie viele Mitarbeiter, Sie eingeschlossen, sind in Ihrem Unternehmen beschäftigt?
Bitte zutreffende Antwort anklicken. Wenn nicht genau bekannt, bitte schätzen.

1. bis 2 Mitarbeiter
2. 3 bis 5 Mitarbeiter
3. 6 bis 9 Mitarbeiter
4. 10 bis 19 Mitarbeiter
5. 20 bis 49 Mitarbeiter
6. 50 bis 99 Mitarbeiter
7. 100 bis 249 Mitarbeiter

A.1.4 Frage S11

Wie hoch ist der Jahresumsatz Ihres Unternehmens? Bitte zutreffende Antwort
anklicken. Wenn nicht genau bekannt, bitte schätzen.

1. Unter 500.000 EUR
2. 500.001 EUR bis 1 Mio. EUR
3. Über 1 Mio. EUR, aber weniger als 5 Mio. EUR
4. Über 5 Mio. EUR, aber weniger als 10 Mio. EUR
5. Über 10 Mio. EUR, aber weniger als 50 Mio. EUR
6. Über 50 Mio. EUR, aber weniger als 100 Mio. EUR
7. Über 100 Mio. EUR, aber weniger als 250 Mio. EUR
8. Über 250 Mio. EUR

A.2 Derzeitige Ausstattung an EDV/IT-Lösungen

A.2.1 Frage G5

Welche Art von EDV/IT Anwendungen setzen Sie in Ihrem Unternehmen ein? Anwendungen für... Bitte alle zutreffenden Antworten anklicken.

1. E-Mail Kommunikation (z.B. Microsoft Outlook, IBM Lotus, Apple Mail)
2. Unified Messaging wie Fax, Chat, Telefonie aus EDV/IT-Lösung, keine herkömmliche Telefonanlage (z.B. Microsoft Lync, IBM Lotus, Google, OpenScape)
3. Textbearbeitung, Tabellenkalkulation und Präsentationen (z.B. Microsoft Office, Google Docs, Lotus, OpenOffice)
4. Projektmanagement (z.B. Microsoft Project, SAP, Primavera, OpenProj)
5. Teamzusammenarbeit (z.B. Microsoft Sharepoint, Skype, Dropbox)
6. Kundenkontaktmanagement bzw. die Kundenpflege - CRM (z.B. Microsoft
   Navision, SAP, Oracle Siebel, Salesforce)
7. Betriebswirtschaftliche Belange, wie Rechnungserstellung, Warenwirtschaft oder
   Finanzbuchhaltung - ERP (z.B. SAP, Oracle, Microsoft, Lexware, WISO)

8. Personalwesen, wie Lohnbuchhaltung, Zeiterfassung etc. (z.B. SAP, Microsoft Dynamics, Oracle)

9. Mobile Aussendienstunterstützung, wie Vertriebsunterstützung, Flottenmanagement etc. (z.B. SAP, Lexware)

10. Anwendungen zur Unterstützung des Einkaufsprozesses (z.B. SAP, Onventis)

11. Web Applications Development (z.B. Adobe Dreamweaver, Microsoft WebMatrix, Google)

12. Sonstiges, und zwar ...

A.2.2 Frage G6/1a, Filter: Frage G5 Pos. 1 (E-Mail Kommunikation) geklickt

Sie haben angegeben, dass Sie Anwendungen für E-Mail Kommunikation nutzen. Welches der folgenden Softwareprodukte nutzen Sie dabei? Bitte zutreffende Antworte anklicken.

1. Microsoft Outlook
2. IBM Lotus Notes
3. Thunderbird
4. KMail
5. Opera
6. Pegasus Mail
7. (Apple) Mail
8. Eudora
9. Google Mail
10. Sonstiges, und zwar ...

A.2.3 Frage G6/2a, Filter: Frage G5 Pos. 2 (Unified Messaging) geklickt

Sie haben angegeben, dass Sie Anwendungen für Unified Messaging nutzen. Welche der folgenden Anwendungen nutzen Sie dabei genau? Bitte zutreffende Antwort anklicken.

1. IBM Lotus Sametime
2. IBM Lotus Domino
3. Microsoft Exchange Server
4. Microsoft Communications Server
5. Microsoft Lync
6. Octopus Desk Unified Communications (Deutsche Telekom)
7. OneBox
8. Google Dienste
9. Aastra
10. OmniTouch (Alcatel-Lucent)

11. Avaya Aura
12. OpenScape (Siemens Enterprise Communication und Microsoft)
13. Cisco Unified Products
14. NEC Univerge Lösung
15. 3COM Unified Messaging
16. Hewlett-Packard Unified Communication and Collaboration-Messaging
17. Nortel CallPilot
18. Oracle Communications Unified Communications
19. Panasonic Unified Communications
20. Interactive Intelligence
21. Mitel
22. Sonstige, und zwar ...

A.2.4 Frage G6/2b , Filter: Frage G5 Pos. 2 (Unified Messaging) geklickt

Welches Feature nutzen Ihre Mitarbeiter am meisten, wenn es um Unified Messaging geht? Bitte zutreffende Antwort anklicken.

1. Instant Messaging
2. Telephonie/VoIP
3. Email
4. Fax
5. Videokonferenz
6. Applikationsharing
7. Location
8. Sonstiges, und zwar ...

A.2.5 Frage G6/3a , Filter: Frage G5 Pos. 3 (Textbearbeitung, Tabellenkalkulation und Präsentationen) geklickt

Sie haben angegeben, dass Sie Anwendungen für Textbearbeitung, Tabellenkalkulation und Präsentationen nutzen. Welche Office-Anwendungen nutzen Sie genau? Bitte zutreffende Antwort anklicken.

1. Microsoft Office
2. Microsoft Works
3. Google Docs
4. Lotus Symphony
5. Lotus SmartSuite
6. StarOffice (Sun)
7. Corel WordPerfect
8. OxygenOffice Professional
9. ZoHo

10. OpenOffice
11. LibreOffice
12. Sonstiges, und zwar ...

A.2.6 Frage G6/4a , Filter: Frage G5 Pos. 4 (Projektmanagement) geklickt

Sie haben angegeben, dass Sie Anwendungen für Projektmanagement nutzen. Welche der folgenden Anwendungen nutzen Sie genau? Bitte zutreffende Antwort anklicken.

1. Microsoft Project
2. SAP RPM
3. Primavera Project Planner
4. OpenProj
5. InLoox
6. Cando
7. Clocking IT
8. Sonstiges, und zwar ...

A.2.7 Frage G6/5a , Filter: Frage G5 Pos. 5 (Teamzusammenarbeit) geklickt

Sie haben angegeben, dass Sie Anwendungen für Teamzusammenarbeit nutzen. Welche der folgenden Anwendungen nutzen Sie genau? Bitte zutreffende Antwort anklicken.

1. Microsoft Sharepoint
2. Google Docs
3. Skype
4. MSN
5. Dropbox
6. TeamBox
7. Staction
8. Zoho Projects
9. activeCollab
10. Klok
11. GroupMind
12. Colabolo
13. Novel GroupWise
14. WorkSpace
15. IBM lotus domino
16. Microsoft Exchange Server
17. Sonstige, und zwar ...

A.2.8 Frage G6/6a , Filter: Frage G5 Pos. 6 (Kundenkontaktmanagement bzw. Kundenpflege - CRM) geklickt

Sie haben angegeben, dass Sie Anwendungen für Kundenkontaktmanagement bzw. Kundenpflege (CRM) nutzen. Welche der folgenden Anwendungen nutzen Sie genau? Bitte zutreffende Antwort anklicken.

1. Microsoft Dynamics NAV
2. SAP CRM
3. Oracle Siebel
4. Salesforce.com
5. Cobra CRM
6. AMTANGEE CRM Software
7. Acabus Plus
8. MX-Contact
9. CAS PIA
10. AVE! Prodatis
11. Daylite
12. Eva/3
13. Sonstige, und zwar ...

A.2.9 Frage G6/7a , Filter: Frage G5 Pos. 7 (Betriebswirtschaftliche Belange) geklickt

Sie haben angegeben, dass Sie Anwendungen für betriebswirtschaftliche Belange wie Rechnungserstellung, Warenwirtschaft und Finanzbuchhaltung - ERP nutzen. Welche der folgenden Anwendungen nutzen Sie genau? Bitte zutreffende Antwort anklicken.

1. SAP
2. Oracle
3. Siebel
4. Microsoft Dynamics AX + NAV
5. SAS
6. Lexware
7. WISO
8. TZ-EasyBuch
9. PSI
10. Abas-Business-Software
11. AvERP
12. inforCOM
13. SAGE
14. Monkey Office

15. EAR 15

16. JobDISPO

17. proALPHA

18. APPlus

19. Epicor

20. SoftM

21. Sonstige, und zwar ...

A.2.10   Frage G6/8a, Filter: Frage G5 Pos. 8 (Personalwesen) geklickt

Sie haben angegeben, dass Sie Anwendungen für Personalwesen nutzen. Welche der folgenden Anwendungen zur Lohnbuchhaltung bzw. Zeiterfassung nutzen Sie genau? Bitte zutreffende Antwort anklicken.

1. SAP

2. Microsoft Dynamics NAV + AX

3. Oracle

4. Siebel

5. SAS

6. Adata Lohn und Gehalt

7. ADDISON

8. ACCENON

9. CHRONOS

10. FOCONIS

11. Lotus

12. LODAS

13. Lexware

14. ATOSS

15. AIDA

16. ARGOS

17. ZEBAU

18. PROMPT

19. Sonstige, und zwar...

A.2.11   Frage G6/9a, Filter: Frage G5 Pos. 9 (Aussendienstunterstützung) geklickt

Sie haben angegeben, dass Sie Anwendungen für mobile Aussendienstunterstützung nutzen. Welche der folgenden Anwendungen nutzen Sie genau? Bitte zutreffende Antwort anklicken.

1. Lexware

2. BüroWARE

3. FABIS
4. Tectura
5. WISO
6. KFZ
7. MonKey
8. Project2web
9. Colib
10. PROMPT
11. Sonstige, und zwar ...

A.2.12 Frage G6/10a, Filter: Frage G5 Pos. 10 (Unterstützung des Einkaufsprozesses) geklickt

Sie haben angegeben, dass Sie Anwendungen für Unterstützung des Einkaufsprozesses nutzen. Welche der folgenden Anwendungen nutzen Sie genau? Bitte zutreffende Antwort anklicken.

1. SAP
2. Onventis
3. Wallmedien
4. Ariba
5. Simple systems
6. CommerceOne
7. Business Mart
8. Pool4tool
9. JCatalog
10. Amicron
11. Lexware
12. Sage
13. Sonstige, und zwar ...

A.2.13 Frage G6/11a, Filter: Frage G5 Pos. 11 (Web Applications Development) geklickt

Sie haben angegeben, dass Sie Anwendungen für Web Applications Development nutzen. Welche der folgenden Anwendungen werden bereits in Ihrem Unternehmen genutzt? Bitte zutreffende Antwort anklicken.

1. Adobe Dreamweaver
2. Adobe Flash
3. Adobe
4. ColdFusion
5. Google

6. Microsoft WebMatrix

7. RapidWeaver

8. WaveMaker

9. ASP.NET

10. CFEclipse

11. Adobe

12. Zend Development

13. Cincom

14. WebORB

15. Sonstige, und zwar ...

A.2.14 Frage G7

Wie werden die Anwendung in Ihrem Unternehmen betrieben? Bitte jeweils zutreffende Antwort anklicken.

1. E-Mail Kommunikation (z.B. Microsoft Outlook, IBM Lotus, Apple Mail)

2. Unified Messaging wie Fax, Chat, Telefonie aus EDV/IT-Lösung, keine herkömmliche Telefonanlage (z.B. Microsoft Lync, IBM Lotus, Google, OpenScape)

3. Textbearbeitung, Tabellenkalkulation und Präsentationen (z.B. Microsoft Office, Google Docs, Lotus, OpenOffice)

4. Projektmanagement (z.B. Microsoft Project, SAP, Primavera, OpenProj)

5. Teamzusammenarbeit (z.B. Microsoft Sharepoint, Skype, Dropbox)

6. Kundenkontaktmanagement bzw. die Kundenpflege - CRM (z.B. Microsoft Navision, SAP, Oracle Siebel, Salesforce)

7. Betriebswirtschaftliche Belange, wie Rechnungserstellung, Warenwirtschaft oder Finanzbuchhaltung - ERP (z.B. SAP, Oracle, Microsoft, Lexware, WISO)

8. Personalwesen, wie Lohnbuchhaltung, Zeiterfassung etc. (z.B. SAP, Microsoft Dynamics, Oracle)

9. Mobile Aussendienstunterstützung, wie Vertriebsunterstützung, Flottenmanagement etc. (z.B. SAP, Lexware)

10. Anwendungen zur Unterstützung des Einkaufsprozesses (z.B. SAP, Onventis)

11. Web Applications Development (z.B. Adobe Dreamweaver, Microsoft WebMatrix, Google)

12. Sonstiges, und zwar...
Antwortmöglichkeiten:

13. Installation auf dem Unternehmensserver mit Clients auf den PC/Notebooks der Mitarbeitern

14. Einzelinstallationen auf den PC/Notebooks der Mitarbeiter

15. Betrieb durch eine EDV/IT Dienstleister ausserhalb des Unternehmensnetzwerks

16. Software as a Service, Cloud Anbieter (z.B. Salesforce)

17. Sonstiges

A.2.15 Frage G8

Welche Art von Support wird von Ihrem jeweiligen Anbieter der verschiedenen Anwendungen angeboten? Bitte jeweils zutreffende Antwort anklicken.

1. E-Mail Kommunikation (z.B. Microsoft Outlook, IBM Lotus, Apple Mail)
2. Unified Messaging wie Fax, Chat, Telefonie aus EDV/IT-Lösung, keine herkömmliche Telefonanlage (z.B. Microsoft Lync, IBM Lotus, Google, OpenScape)
3. Textbearbeitung, Tabellenkalkulation und Präsentationen (z.B. Microsoft Office, Google Docs, Lotus, OpenOffice)
4. Projektmanagement (z.B. Microsoft Project, SAP, Primavera, OpenProj)
5. Teamzusammenarbeit (z.B. Microsoft Sharepoint, Skype, Dropbox)
6. Kundenkontaktmanagement bzw. die Kundenpflege - CRM (z.B. Microsoft Navision, SAP, Oracle Siebel, Salesforce)
7. Betriebswirtschaftliche Belange, wie Rechnungserstellung, Warenwirtschaft oder Finanzbuchhaltung - EHP (z.B. SAP, Oracle, Microsoft, Lexware, WISO)
8. Personalwesen, wie Lohnbuchhaltung, Zeiterfassung etc. (z.B. SAP, Microsoft Dynamics, Oracle)
9. Mobile Aussendienstunterstützung, wie Vertriebsunterstützung, Flottenmanagement etc. (z.B. SAP, Lexware)
10. Anwendungen zur Unterstützung des Einkaufsprozesses (z.B. SAP, Onventis)
11. Web Applications Development (z.B. Adobe Dreamweaver, Microsoft WebMatrix, Google)
12. Sonstiges, und zwar

A.2.15.1 Antwortmöglichkeiten:

1. Telefonisch
2. Vor-Ort
3. Remote
4. Sonstiges

A.2.16 Frage G10

Wie zufrieden sind Sie mit den derzeitigen EDV/IT Anwendungen insgesamt? Bitte zutreffende Antwort anklicken.

1. äusserst zufrieden
2. Sehr zufrieden
3. Zufrieden
4. Eher unzufrieden
5. Überhaupt nicht zufrieden

A.2.17 Frage G11, Filter: G10 Pos. 1-2

Warum sind Sie mit Ihren derzeitigen Anwendungen so zufrieden? Bitte schreiben Sie alles auf, was Ihnen hierzu einfällt. Bitte Antworten möglichst detailliert eingeben.

A.2.18 Frage G12, Filter: G10 Pos. 3-5

Warum sind Sie mit Ihren derzeitigen Anwendungen eher nicht zufrieden? Bitte schreiben Sie alles auf, was Ihnen hierzu einfällt. Bitte Antworten möglichst detailliert eingeben.

A.2.19 Frage G13

Könnten Sie sich vorstellen, Cloud-Services zu nutzen, damit sind bspw. Anwendungen gemeint, die nicht mehr bei Ihnen installiert sind, sondern von einem Anbieter bereitgestellt werden und über einen Internetanschluss erreichbar sind? Bitte zutreffende Antwort anklicken.

1. Ich habe noch nicht von einem Cloud Service gehört
2. Cloud Services kommt in unserem Unternehmen nicht in Frage
3. Cloud Services kommt in unserem Unternehmen in Frage, die Anschaffung ist aber nicht geplant
4. Die Anschaffung Cloud Services ist in nächster Zeit geplant
5. Wir nutzen Cloud Services bereits in unserem Unternehmen

A.2.20 Frage G14, Filter: Frage G13 Pos. 3-4 geklickt ("kommt in Frage"/ "in nächster Zeit geplant")

In welchem Zeitrahmen wird in Ihrem Unternehmen an die Einführung von Cloud Services gedacht? Bitte zutreffende Antwort anklicken.

1. Sofort
2. 1-3 Monate
3. 3-6 Monate
4. 6 Monate- 1 Jahr
5. 1 Jahr-2 Jahre
6. >2 Jahre

A.2.21 Frage G15 , Filter: Frage G13 Pos. 3-5 geklickt ("kommt in Frage"/ "in nächster Zeit geplant"/"wird bereits genutzt")

Welche Art von Cloud Services nutzen bzw. planen Sie zu nutzen? Bitte zutreffende Antwort anklicken.

1. SaaS - "Software as a Service"
2. PaaS - "Platform as a Service"

3. IaaS - "Infrastructure as a Service" (z.B Storage, Computing power)
4. Sonstiges, und zwar ...

Antwortmöglichkeiten:

1. Wird bereits genutzt
2. Nutzung ist geplant
3. Nutzung ist nicht geplant

A.2.22 Frage G16, Filter: Frage G15_1 Pos. 1-2 ("SaaS wird bereits genutzt", "Nutzung ist geplant")

Welche Art von "Software as a Service" planen Sie in nächster Zeit anzuschaffen? Bitte jeweils nach zutreffender Wichtigkeit anklicken.

1. E-Mail Kommunikation
2. Unified Messaging wie Fax, Chat, Telefonie
3. Textbearbeitung, Tabellenkalkulation und Präsentationen
4. Projektmanagement
5. Teamzusammenarbeit
6. Kundenkontaktmanagement bzw. die Kundenpflege - CRM
7. Betriebswirtschaftliche Belange, wie Rechnungserstellung, Warenwirtschaft oder Finanzbuchhaltung)
8. Personalwesen, wie Lohnbuchhaltung, Zeiterfassung etc.
9. Mobile Aussendienstunterstützung, wie Vertriebsunterstützung, Flottenmanagement etc.
10. Anwendungen zur Unterstützung des Einkaufsprozesses
11. Absicherung des Unternehmensnetzes wie Firewall, Intrusion Prevention, Antivirensoftware /E-Mail-Schutz
12. Sonstiges, und zwar ...

Antwortmöglichkeiten:

1. Am wichtigsten
2. Am zweitwichtigsten
3. Am drittwichtigsten
4. Am viertwichtigsten

A.2.23 Frage G21, Filter: Frage G15_3 Pos. 1 ("IaaS wird bereits genutzt")

Welche Art von IaaS - "Infrastructure as a Service" nutzen Sie? Bitte zutreffende Antwort anklicken.

1. Im Bereich Speicher (Storage)
2. Im Bereich Rechenleistung (Computing / processing power)
3. Sonstiges, und zwar ...

A.2.24 Frage G22, Filter: Frage G13 Pos. 3-5 geklickt ("kommt in Frage"/ "in nächster Zeit geplant"/ "wird bereits genutzt")

Bitte beschreiben Sie die Cloud Services näher, die für Sie in Frage kommen, die Sie nutzen bzw. planen? Bitte nennen Sie auch insbesondere den Anbieter. Bitte schreiben Sie alles auf, was Ihnen hierzu einfällt. Bitte Antworten möglichst detailliert eingeben.

A.2.25 Frage G23, Filter: Frage G13 Pos. 3-5 geklickt ("kommt in Frage"/ "in nächster Zeit geplant"/ "wird bereits genutzt")

Wer ist für Sie der ideale Anbieter für die zuvor beschriebenen Cloud Services? Bitte zutreffende Antwort anklicken.

1. Großer amerikanischer Anbieter
2. Großer deutscher Anbieter
3. über einen regionalen IT Partner /IT-Systemhaus
4. über einen überregionalen Anbieter
5. über den Anbieter der Branchensoftware
6. über einen IT-Händler/Distributor
7. Sonstiges, und zwar ...

A.2.26 Frage G24, Filter: Frage G13 Pos. 3-5 geklickt ("kommt in Frage""in nächster Zeit geplant""wird bereits genutzt")

Denken Sie dabei an einen bestimmten Anbieter? Würden Sie uns diesen bitte nennen? Bitte Antworten möglichst detailliert eingeben.

A.2.27 Frage G25, Filter: Frage G13 Pos. 3-4 geklickt ("kommt in Frage"/"in nächster Zeit geplant")

Welche der folgenden Aspekte wären Ihnen wichtig, wenn Sie nach einem Anbieter für Cloud Services suchen würden? Bitte wählen Sie die 5 wichtigsten Kriterien aus! Bitte zutreffende Antwort anklicken.

1. Marktführerschaft des Anbieters / Größe des Anbieters
2. Niedrige Kosten
3. Kostentransparenz
4. Datenstandort in Deutschland
5. Firmenhauptsitz in Deutschland
6. Sicherheitsaspekte
7. Verträge und SLA (Service Level Agreements) nach deutschen Recht
8. Deutschsprachigen Kundenservice (telefonisch, schriftlich)
9. Kundenservice in Deutschland (persönlich)

10. Regelmäßige Prüfung von Rechenzentrum und Ablaufprozesse durch zertifizierte Security-Auditors (z.B. TüV)
11. Zertifizierte Mitarbeiter
12. Kundenreferenzen
13. Anpassungsmöglichkeit / Kundenspezifisches Produkt
14. Support bei der Prüfung von Betriebskosten-Senkung
15. Unterstützung bei Einführung und Migration der Altsysteme
16. Kompatibilität der Anwendung zu bestehenden Systemen
17. Schulung
18. Sonstiges, und zwar...

A.2.28 Frage G26, Filter: Frage G13 Pos. 1-4 geklickt ("noch nichts von Cloud gehört"/"kommt nicht in Frage"/"kommt in Frage"/"in nächster Zeit geplant")

Was sind Ihrer Meinung nach die Hauptgründe, die gegen eine Einführung von Cloud Services sprechen könnten? Bitte wählen Sie die 5 wichtigsten Gründen aus! Bitte zutreffende Antwort anklicken.

1. Kein Mehrwert
2. Hohe Entwicklungsaufwand
3. Hohe Initialkosten
4. Hohe Migrationskosten
5. Sicherheitsbedenken
6. Geringe Verfügbarkeit von Mitarbeiter / IT Kompetenz nicht vorhanden
7. Geringe Kompatibilität mit bestehenden Systemen / Anwendungen
8. Geringes Vertrauen zu neue Technologien
9. Die notwendigen Investitionen wären zu hoch
10. Datenschutz bzw. -missbrauch
11. Datensicherheitsbedenken
12. IT-Kompetenzverlust
13. Geringe Verfügbarkeit und Netzgeschwindigkeit
14. Neue Abhängigkeit von Cloud-Anbietern
15. Proprietäre Lösungen
16. Kein Vertrauen in Cloud-Anwendungen
17. Fehlende Preis-Transparenz
18. Kostenentwicklung nicht planbar
19. Zuverlässigkeit des Internets
20. Sonstiges, und zwar ...

LIST OF FIGURES

LIST OF ABBREVIATIONS

CAD	Computer-aided design
CC	Cloud Computing
CRM	Customer Relationship Management
DAX	German stock index (Deutscher Aktien IndeX)
EDV	Electronic Data Processing
ERP	Enterprise Resource Planning
HR	Human Resources
HTML	Hypertext Markup Language
IaaS	Infrastructure as a Service
IAO	Institute for work management and organization
IBM	International Business Machines Corporation
ICT	Information and communications technology
IDS	Intrusion detection system
IPS	Intrusion prevention system
IT	Information Technology
MBA	Master of Business Administration
MDM	Mobile Device Management
MS	Microsoft Corporation
MSN	Microsoft Messenger
NIST	National Institute of Standards and Technology
p.	Page
PaaS	Platform as a Service
PAYG	Pay-as-you-go
PC	Personal Computer
PIMS	Profit Impact of Marketing Strategy
pp.	Pages
SaaS	Software as a Service
SAP	Systems, Applications and Products in Data Processing AG
SLA	Service Level Agreement
SMB	Small and Medium sized business
SOA	Service-oriented Architecture
SWOT	Strengths, Weaknesses, Opportunities and Threats
TCO	Total Cost of Ownership
TÜV	Technischer Überwachungs-Verein
USA	United States of America
UTM	Unified Threat Management
VoIP	Voice over Internet Protocol

BIBLIOGRAPHY

[1] Baun, Christian; Kunze, Marcel: *Cloud computing: Web-basierte dynamische IT-Services.* Springer, 2010.

[2] Buzzel, Robert D.: *The PIMS program of strategy research. A retrospective appraisal.* Journal of Business Research, 57, 2004, pp. 478-483

[3] European Union: *Commission recommendation concerning the definition of micro, small and medium-sized enterprise.* Official Journal, 2003

[4] Grant, Robert M.: *Contemporary strategy analysis.* Fourth edition, Blackwell publishing, 2002

[5] Hofer, Chuck; Schendel, Dan: *Strategy formulation: Analytical concepts.* St. Paul: West Publishing, 1977

[6] Hoffmann, Mario: *Sicher in der Cloud.* University Journal, 12. volume, April-Mai, 2011

[7] Köhler-Schute, Christiana; et al: *Cloud Computing: Neue Optionen für Unternehmen.* KS Energy Verlag, 2011

[8] Kretschmer, Tobias: *Vernetztes Arbeiten in Wirtschaft und Gesellschaft.* 2010

[9] Holtkamp, Berndhard: *Cloud Computing für den Mittelstand am Beispiel der Logistikbranche.* Fraunhofer ISST, 2010

[10] Metzger, Christian; Reitz, Thorsten; Villar, Juan: *Cloud computing, Chancen und Risiken aus technischer und unternehmerischer Sicht.* Hanser, 2011

[11] Möller, Christian: *Diplomarbeit mit dem Thema Cloud Computing-Einsatz im E-Business.* Grin, 2010

[12] Oetiker, Tobias: *The not so short introduction to LaTeX.* 2011

[13] Porter, Michael E.: *The five competitive forces that shape strategy.* Harvard Business Review, volume January, 2008, p. 4

[14] Rhoton, John: *Cloud Computing Explained.* Recursive Press, 2010

[15] Terplan, Kornel; Voigt, Christian: *Cloud Computing.* mitp, 2011

[16] T-Systems Enterprise Services: *White Paper. Cloud Computing I.* T-Systems, 2011

[17] T-Systems Enterprise Services: *White Paper. Cloud Computing II.* T-Systems, 2011

[18] T-Systems Enterprise Services: *White Paper. Dynamic Services.* T-Systems, 2011

[19] Van Zütphen, Thomas: *Avancen aus der Wolke.* Best Practice - Das Kundenmagazin von T-Systems, volume 01, 2011, pp. 18-21

[20] Van Zütphen, Thomas: *Der CIO als Cloud-Broker.* Das Kundenmagazin von T-Systems, volume 01, 2011, pp. 22-23

[21] Velte, Anthony; Velte, Toby; Elsenpeter, Robert: *Cloud computing: A practical approach.* McGrawHill, 2010

[22] Wamser, Christoph: *Strategisches Electronic Commerce.* Verlag Vahlen, 2001

[23] Weidmann, Monika; Renner, Thomas; Rex, Sascha: *Cloud computing in der Versicherungsbranche.* Fraunhofer IAO, 2010.

Internet sources

[24] Bias, Randy: *Debunking the "No Such Thing as A Private Cloud" Myth,* January 19, 2010. Retrieved February 20, 2012, from http://www.cloudscaling.com/blog/cloud-computing/debunking-the-no-such-thing-as-a-private-cloud-myth

[25] Cloud puzzle: *Cloud Puzzle Online Applications and Services Directory,* 2012. Retrieved November 19, 2011, from http://www.cloudpuzzle.com

[26] ERP software: *Der Größte unabhängige ERP-Software Vergleich,* 2011. Retrieved November 26, 2011, from http://www.erp-software.org/erp-software-finden

[27] Forrester Research: *Cloud computing definition,* 2011. Retrieved February 12, 2012, from http://www.forrester.com/rb/research

[28] Gartner Research: *Gartner Says Worldwide Cloud Services Market to Surpass $68 Billion in 2010,* June 22, 2010. Retrieved March 4, 2012, from http://www.gartner.com/it/page.jsp?id=1389313

[29] Gartner research: *Gartner says cloud computing will be as influential as E-business,* June 26, 2008. Retrieved February 12, 2012, from http://www.gartner.com/it/page.jsp?id=707508

[30] Göldi, Andreas: *Google macht Ernst mit Cloud Computing,* March 11, 2010. Retrieved November 26, 2011, from ttp://netzwertig.com/2010/03/11/app-marketplace-google-macht-ernst-mit-enterprise-cloud-computing

[31] Google: *Google Apps for Business,* 2012. Retrieved November 26, 2011, from http://www.google.com/apps/intl/en/business/index.html

[32] Google: *Google Apps Marketplace,*2011. Retrieved November 27, 2011, from http://www.google.com/enterprise/marketplace

[33] Grohmann, Werner: *Initiative Cloud Services Made in Germany*, 2011. Retrieved November 19, 2011, from `http://www.cloud-services-made-in-germany.de`

[34] IBM corporation: *Unified communications*, 2012. Retrieved March 12, 2012, from `http://www-142.ibm.com/software/products/us/en/category/SWAAA`

[35] Microsoft corporation: *SMB Value, Journey to the Cloud*, 2011. Retrieved February 19, 2012, from `http://www.microsoft.com/business/Office365/webcasts/smb-value-journey-to-the-cloud.asp`

[36] National Institute of Standards and Technology: *NIST Definition of Cloud Computing*, 2011. Retrieved November 19, 2011, from `http://csrc.nist.gov/publications/nistpubs/800-145/SP800-145.pdf`

[37] Open projects software: *Software definition*, 2012. Retrieved March 12, 2012, from `http://www.openprojects.org/software-definition.htm`

[38] PC magazine encyclopedia: *Definition of client/server*, 2012. Retrieved March 4, 2012, from `http://www.pcmag.com/encyclopedia_term/0,2542,t=clientserver&i=39801,00.asp`

[39] PC magazine encyclopedia: *Definition of cloud computing*, 2012. Retrieved March 4, 2012, from `http://www.pcmag.com/encyclopedia`

[40] PC magazine encyclopedia: *Web development software*, 2012. Retrieved March 12, 2012, from `http://www.pcmag.com/encyclopedia_term/0,2542,t=Web+development+software&i=54296,00.asp`

[41] Project management software: *Project management software*, 2011. Retrieved March 12, 2012, from `http://www.projectmanagementsoftware.com`

[42] Salesforce: *The cloud computing marketplace from Salesforce*, 2011. Retrieved November 26, 2011, from `http://appexchange.salesforce.com/home`

[43] Techopedia: *Application suite*, 2012. Retrieved March 12, 2012, from `http://www.techopedia.com/definition/4224/application-software`

[44] Webopedia, IT Business Edge: *Application software definition*, 2012. Retrieved March 12, 2012, from `http://www.webopedia.com/TERM/A/application.html`

[45] Webopedia, IT Business Edge: *Customer relationship management software*, 2012. Retrieved March 12, 2012, from `http://www.webopedia.com/TERM/C/CRM.html`

[46] Webopedia, IT Business Edge: *Enterprise Resource Planning*, 2012. Retrieved March 12, 2012, from `http://www.webopedia.com/TERM/E/ERP.html`

[47] Webopedia, IT Business Edge: *What is mainframe?*, 2012. Retrieved March 4, 2012, from http://www.webopedia.com/TERM/M/mainframe.html

[48] Wikipedia: *Client-server model*, 2012. Retrieved March 4, 2012, from http://en.wikipedia.org/wiki/Client-server_model

[49] Wikipedia: *Cloud Computing*, 2012. Retrieved February 2, 2012, from http://en.wikipedia.org/wiki/Cloud_computing

[50] Wikipedia: *Communication software*, 2012. Retrieved March 8, 2012, from http://en.wikipedia.org/wiki/Communication_software

[51] Wikipedia: *Fleet management software*, 2012. Retrieved March 14, 2012, from http://en.wikipedia.org/wiki/Fleet_management_software

[52] Wikipedia: *Grossrechner*, 2012. Retrieved March 4, 2012, from http://de.wikipedia.org/wiki/Grossrechner

[53] Wikipedia: *Human resource management system*, 2012. Retrieved March 14 2012, from http://en.wikipedia.org/wiki/Human_resource_management_system

[54] Wikipedia: *Mittelstand*, 2012. Retrieved March 12 2012, from http://en.wikipedia.org/wiki/Mittelstand

[55] Wikipedia: *Procurement software*, 2012. Retrieved March 12, 2012, from http://en.wikipedia.org/wiki/Procurement_software

[56] Wikipedia: *Team collaboration software*, 2012. Retrieved March 12, 2012, from http://en.wikipedia.org/wiki/Collaborative_software